UNCOVERING T[...]
BEHIND PORN

UNCOVERING THE TRUTH
BEHIND PORN

# THE DIRTY LITTLE
# SECRET

WITH CARTER KRUMMRICH

# CRAIG GROSS

FOUNDER OF XXXCHURCH.COM

ZONDERVAN™

GRAND RAPIDS, MICHIGAN 49530 USA

ZONDERVAN.COM/
AUTHORTRACKER

We want to hear from you. Please send your comments about this book to us in care of zreview@zondervan.com. Thank you.

**ZONDERVAN™**

*The Dirty Little Secret*
Copyright © 2006 by Craig Gross

Requests for information should be addressed to:
Zondervan, *Grand Rapids, Michigan 49530*

---

Library of Congress Cataloging-in-Publication Data

Gross, Craig.
  The dirty little secret : uncovering the truth behind porn / Craig Gross with Carter Krummrich.
    p. cm.
  ISBN-13: 978-0-310-27107-9
  ISBN-10: 0-310-27107-X
  1. Pornography. 2. Pornography—Religious aspects—Christianity. I. Krummrich, Carter. II. Title.
  HQ471.G76 2006
  261.8'3577—dc22                                    2005034021

---

Note that most names in this book do not have last names, and many have been changed so that their identity cannot be determined.

The website addresses recommended throughout this book are offered as a resource to you. These websites are not intended in any way to be or imply an endorsement on the part of Zondervan, nor do we vouch for their content for the life of this book.

Published in association with Yates & Yates, LLP, Attorneys and Counselors, Orange, California.

*Interior design by Michelle Espinoza*

*Printed in the United States of America*

---

06 07 08 09 10 11 12 • 18 17 16 15 14 13 12 11 10 9 8 7 6 5 4 3 2 1

*To Josh and Michelle*
*Thanks for inspiring me with your trust*
*and honesty and vulnerability.*
*May you draw near to each other and draw close to God.*
*May you enjoy your new life together.*

# THE PORN PASTOR

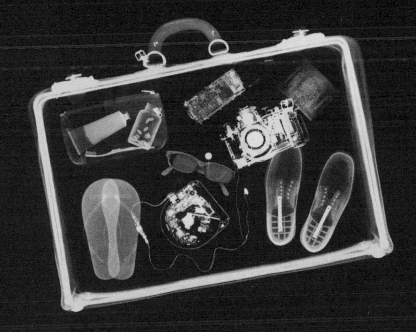

It was a stupid thing to do, but I did it anyway. I turned my car into the "Porn Mobile." I painted my website domain XXXchurch. com and the slogan "#1 Christian Porn Site" all over my black Scion XB in big, bold-faced letters. On the passenger door is the wording "A porn site for the whole family." The car is unavoidable. I drive it on the freeway and roads where I live in Riverside County, California, garnering stares from just about everybody. The words cover the entire car, running from the driver side door all the way to the back. At the time, I was excited. The design schematic and graphics were high quality, and I was so excited that I called all my friends and drove my new ride to their houses to show it off. This is the car I had been driving to buy groceries for my family and to visit friends. Now I think back to my rash decision and smile. Would I do it again? Probably.

I first realized something was wrong when the driver of the car next to me threw his milk shake onto my windshield. A thirty-two ounce soda came the following week. People either gave me a thumbs-up or the bird. How could a simple gesture such as putting the word *porn* on the outside of a car generate such a big response? I can't drive anywhere without somebody running up to me and asking what the car is about, or telling me how they have struggled with porn. Azusa Pacific, a Christian university, almost had the car towed from their parking lot. Even my wife doesn't want the car parked in our driveway, so I keep it covered.

Last month, I lent the car to my friend Dave because his broke down. In that month, a Christian driver waved a Bible at him from the road and visibly prayed for his soul. His best friend, an artist, hid behind his sculpture in town because Dave waved to him from the Porn Mobile. Dave's wife wouldn't drive it at all. He had even been threatened by the police with a misdemeanor for taking pictures of the car for our website.

Later, I realized that I had turned my car into a hot-button issue. What I have learned from driving around a car with the word *porn* all over it is that people don't want to talk about this issue. The word makes people nervous, afraid, uncomfortable, and excited.

## PORN

Here's an experiment: Say the word *porn* at a dinner party sometime and see what happens. Depending on what kind of dinner party you're at, you are more than likely to be confronted with blank stares, nervous twitching of hands, sweating brows, and anxious laughter. Some might spill their drinks and others will leap through flaming hoops to be first to change the subject. For the rest of the night, they'll avoid you and probably won't invite you back to the next gathering. Four years ago, I would have had the exact same reaction. Being a pastor doesn't change any of this; I would have avoided that trip to the porn gutter at all costs. This was my subconscious attempt to pass over the issue as if it didn't exist. To me, porn was a dark world inhabited by lost sinners selling their bodies and souls over to a flesh-driven abomination.

Try telling this to me now, four years into my strange and remarkable journey with the XXXchurch. In fact, the very word that makes people fidget or sweat has become part of my title. Media sources like CNN, *The 700 Club*, and *The Daily Show* have dubbed my partner, Mike Foster, and I the "porn pastors." We are the creators of the XXXchurch, a ministry that confronts porn on two levels—that of the church and that of the porn industry. The seedy and the sacred—a hybrid of the world we represent and the world we inhabit, despite the misgivings of many Christians and the animosity of those in the porn business.

So what am I? A pastor? A pornographer? You might not believe it, but Mike and I are ordained ministers. We can do weddings and funerals and have the certificates to prove it. You wouldn't know it by looking at me. At age twenty-nine, I still dress as if I belong at the skate park. I'm a generation gap, black earrings, cargo pants, youth culture, long hair, SoCal, skate shoes kind of guy. You could say your average grandmother wouldn't approve, though mine does.

I am married with two kids and live in a suburban house. My son is two years old, and I have a newborn baby girl. My wife has gotten used to some of the people I surround myself with and work with, but I don't think she'll ever get used to the car.

Strange that I find my calling is to battle porn. Why should we even battle it? If you watch or read a lot of Christian material on the subject, you'll hear "Just don't do it!" As if becoming a Christian suddenly erases a man's or woman's drive to look at porn. Then there is the Christian notion that porn is a pastime of only the sinful and wicked. Pornographers and porn consumers fit somewhere between liberals and homosexuals on the scale of Christian good and evil. What about the stripper who needs to support her children? What about the pastor who has a secret addiction to porn? What about the pornographer who wishes he could erase some of what he has seen and done because it haunts him at night? The issue is a little more complicated than good and evil, black and white. The human being is a hazardous jumble of wires, not the strong cables we like to think of ourselves as.

I didn't always see everybody as so complex, and I'll admit, sometimes I still don't. Sometimes I look at someone in this business or the Christian world and think, "I'm right; you're wrong." Or, "I'm better than you. How can you live with yourself?" This is my natural tendency, but I'm getting better at catching myself.

I'm getting better at showing grace where before, there was only judgment. I remember one such instance clearly.

## BLACK STREAMERS

One balmy night in Pomona, I walked into a convenience store during a late hour to buy a soda. Aisles of the usual pastry snacks and health bars covered the small store, like thousands upon thousands of convenience and liquor stores everywhere. The clerk looked up from a book to give me a customary nod and his eyes fell back to the pages. Because of the hour, I was the only customer. I walked across the worn tile to the refrigerators near the wall and grabbed my 7UP.

Suddenly a small, furtive man wearing a ruffled jacket over a collared shirt entered to the sound of the beeping sensors. He quickly made his way toward the back of the store and stopped in a small nook hidden away in the farthest corner. I could barely make out the man searching through whatever merchandise that back corner held. He could have been anybody, a blue-collar construction worker, a businessman getting back late from the office, a waiter, a teacher, a husband, a father. His face held nothing, not even a satisfied gesture once he found his desired good. The man positioned his body to hide the item and pulled it out for the clerk, keeping his head down, not saying a word. The clerk scanned what looked like a magazine in a shiny plastic cover, put it in a bag, and handed it back to the man. He paid with exact change and left, walking briskly.

By that time, I had a pretty good idea what the man had just bought. Still, my curious nature got the best of me, and I made my way back to the hidden corner. I turned into the alcove and shelves full of magazines and videos confronted my vision, except I couldn't see any of the covers. Attached to the shelves were long

black streamers made out of industrial trash bags. The streamers provided a buffer for my eyes. In order to access the hidden pornography, I would have to reach through the black wall
of streamers. Just then, another customer came through the door
and a breeze ruffled the streamers; my eyes caught a glimpse
of exposed flesh. So this was what the man had been browsing
through, dipping his hands through the layer of streamers and
choosing which porn he'd take home that night. So I dismissed
the man and felt sorry for him. I adopted a "holier than thou"
attitude.

As I look back on this incident, I feel ashamed. A painful
memory came back to me of my close friend, a youth pastor who
was fired for looking at porn. How did I know the small, furtive
man wasn't a Christian or even a pastor? I was so ready to count
him among the unbelievers and not show him any grace. This is
the danger of porn to the church. We are so used to the black
wall of streamers blocking our vision that we forget the dangerous addictions found within the flimsy barrier. So many believers
and Christian pastors have their hands within these dangerous
boundaries and don't know how to withdraw them. We ignore the
problem while people struggle inside. We need a wake-up call, a
call strong enough to rustle the streamers and show Christians
that this problem exists. And if it takes a car that makes a few
people uncomfortable, then so be it.

## XXXCHURCH

You can call the XXXchurch a journey—my journey. A better
way to describe it is a headfirst dive into a pit full of jellyfish. Every
journey has a beginning. Four years ago the word *pornography*
brought cursory images to my mind, the bare surface of a world I
knew nothing about. My mind conjured up sleazy producers and

porn stars filming perversities, but the filming and producing were miles upon miles away from my own home. Four years ago, I hadn't the slightest clue I'd bring the issue home with me.

So what happened four years ago? Did I suddenly get a degree in "pornology"? No, my friend and fellow pastor Mike Foster was taking a shower one morning when God whispered the word *porn* to him. It was that simple. He came to me because he knew I was the kind of guy who took ideas and actually followed through on them. We rationalized that nobody was talking about this issue and something needed to be said. We're not ex-porno addicts and we don't have the story of hitting rock bottom. We simply saw a void and envisioned ourselves filling it.

Yes, Mike felt God had spoken just the single word to him while he showered one morning. That word. That single, dirty, ugly, yucky, filthy word that we just don't talk about in church. But what were we supposed to do with it? We began to brainstorm ideas, and eventually decided right then and there to start a website and to call it XXXchurch.com. We even came up with our tagline—"The #1 Christian Porn Site"—right there on the spot.

In the midst of our excitement that day, somber memories bombarded me. Even though I didn't have the incredible story of surviving porn, I had a few friends who did. I started thinking again about my good friend who lost his job as a youth pastor because of a few run-ins with porn. I thought about an elder from my church who lost his wife and family over his ten-year battle with porn. And I thought about a woman I'd met whose marriage was annulled after just a few short months because of porn.

I attacked this issue with a bittersweet drive, fueled by the pain of those I loved falling on this deadly battleground and tempered by the revelation that I, Craig Gross, with the help of God, had the power to change it. I distinctly remember that nervous race back to my office so we could register the domain name, hoping no one had it—and fortunately no one did. It wasn't long before we made T-shirts and stickers ... and we had no clue what we were doing, other than knowing we had to help guys who liked to look at naked women in the secrecy of their homes and offices and didn't want to talk about it. As time went by, we discovered that even women and young kids had problems with porn.

We hadn't studied the issue of porn but felt a calling too strong to ignore. It was such a dirty little secret. So on January 9, 2002, XXXchurch.com made its internet debut, and boy were we blown away by the response. At first, however, we only had two words on our website: "Porn Sucks." Mike and I sat in my office staring at the words for five minutes, a boyish grin lit up Mike's face. There seemed to be a simple truth to them. Yeah, porn sucks. We knew we needed more, so we started going to other websites and stealing their statistics on porn. Hey, everyone needs a little inspiration.

After rearranging the content a few times, we felt that we needed to find the real face of porn. We began to go out in public and interview people, classic "man on the street" style testimony. It was a hit almost immediately, and suddenly we had a lot of exposure. January 9, the day we started our journey, held a darker omen. The date was the opening day of the AVN Adult Expo in Las Vegas, Nevada, the largest pornography trade show in the United States. Strange coincidence? Maybe. We decided the fight would be held there, at the front lines, taking our calling from behind the computer screen and our website domain to the very hive and lifeblood of the industry. But what kind of battle would we choose to fight?

We didn't know what the porn industry would think of us, because they're constantly under attack, and not just by religious groups. But we decided early on not to fight against the industry as such; instead, we went in with a completely different approach: we went to their turf on their terms. And because we took the first step, the people in the industry got to know us. And once they got to know us, we started hearing them say, "You guys aren't like the other religious people; you aren't what we thought of as Christians."

How can this be? It's simple: we're honest about our profession, about our faith, and about our humanity. The porn industry and the secular culture have embraced us. Not that everyone gives us big high fives every time they see us, but on the whole, we have encountered astonishingly little resistance from the industry because deep down, they are all just sinners like you and me, desperately looking for someone to love them. And that's what we do. Since we started XXXchurch, we have had a ton of opportunities to get an insider's look at the world of porn, and we always bring honesty with us. Both Christians and non-Christians struggle with the issue of pornography, so we take the real life approach, step back from all that's been said about it, and come at it straightforwardly and honestly. And controversially.

This is the world I've chosen to live in. We're trying to help people see the true nature of pornography. It's pure exploitation, the objectification of sex. God gave us so much more than that. Christianity doesn't condemn sex or pleasure. Sex is a wonderful gift fully sanctified in God's glory. Have you ever read Song of Solomon? Ever wonder what that little piece of erotic writing is doing in the Bible? Yet we choose to ignore this gift for something much more carnal; we wolf down the cheeseburger and fries when we're offered the filet minon. That's just what porn is: sex packaged in a fast-food wrapper, dumbed down and exploited for profit and mass consumption.

## THE PORN PASTOR

So is this just another book about porn then? Another voice yelling that porn sucks and you're a sinner if you consume it? Another voice condemning the likes of Jenna Jameson and the rest of her profession? Not exactly. We can preach about the negative effects of porn all day, and that's precisely what many people in the church choose to do when it comes to sexuality. But that's the problem.

What's the first image that pops in your head when you hear the words *church* and *porn* together? Probably that of a stern minister wagging a condemning finger. We wanted to change that and decided the only way we could change something was if we got out there among the people and took a look at what was going on in the world of porn. No, I'm not going to preach, but I'd like to introduce you to a few of the people in my world, the world of the Porn Pastor.

There are so many facts and statistics available on pornography, but the biggest fact of all is that none of these stats will keep people away from porn. As the Porn Pastor, I have headed out on a journey and tried to put a human face on the side of porn. I am not an expert; my degree is not in sexual addiction, but I love people and see pornography as a deadly threat to the individual. I have met porn stars, porn producers, prostitutes, porn addicts, and many other lost people. The crazy thing is a lot of those people at one time looked just like you and me. A lot of those people still look just like you and me.

You're about to meet several people I have met. Some you may consider extreme examples, while others are stories from soccer moms and seminary students. The media and the entertainment industry paints this rosy picture of the porn industry every day. What they don't tell you are the stories of the countless abused girls on the porn sets or the broken marriages of men and women who choose porn. Desensitized humans wrapped up in sexual fantasies, alone in their addictions. Family members who are crushed when they discover the secret.

```
Hello,
    I have found pornography on my father's
computer numerous times over the past 3-5
years. My father is a pastor in a church,
making this behavior even more difficult to
swallow (although I know this is a common
act in pastors). Do you have any suggestions
on how to confront/approach my father about
this?
    Thank you,
    Kerrie
```

My inbox is full of letters as I sit at my computer to read. Kerrie's email hits especially close to home. You just don't think of pastors in the church as being addicted to porn. They are people you go to with struggles; they comfort you when you hurt. What do I tell this girl? How do you advise a daughter to confront her father about porn? Could this have been me with my own daughter finding porn on my computer years later if I had done things differently? What if my road as a pastor had turned out this way?

This was the road taken by two of my fellow college graduates at Hope International University, both of them fired from their ministry jobs for an incident involving porn. Rather than help them with their struggles, the church chose to terminate them. This could have been me, but I escaped. My story with porn is about dodging a bullet. I'm still human. I don't have a "get out of porn penitentiary free" card with my pastor credentials. I'll tell you that even now, with a wife and two kids, I could log onto a porn website tomorrow.

People see me on the news doing crazy things, like setting up an xxxchurch booth at porn shows with our gimmicks. The first year we had Rex the Rabbit, a big friendly version of the Playboy bunny. Various people we knew would don our life-size rabbit costume and give porn stars hugs. Skeptics ask, "How come you can go to all these things and not be affected by it?" That's the great paradox: I'm still human and have the same drives as everybody else; however, I make sure I'm prepared before I go. I don't walk into a porn convention lightly. In fact, most of the time, my wife is in the rabbit costume. I'm not going to ogle porn stars or linger at other booths because I know she's watching and I know a number of people helping out at the booth are with me at all times. When I'm alone or in a weak state, I know I have X3watch accountability software on my computer and close friends I can call and be honest with the situation.

Growing up before the internet, you had to be lucky as I was to stumble across porn, steal it, or find your dad's secret stash. For me, those few pages ripped from a magazine sat in between my Michael Jordan rookie card and my 1986 Tops Traded Set. For a while, it was my only outlet. I eventually threw them away after hearing that you could see free porn on TV even if your parents did not subscribe to all the nasty channels. All you had to do was fiddle with two specific buttons on the remote control. Then, all of a sudden, it would descramble the porn. Hours went by trying this technique. I was convinced I saw porn, but it still wasn't real clear.

One time in junior high, my friends and I found a magazine on the track at school and hid it in my friend Scott's locker. Scott divvied up a few pages to each of us and hid the rest in his garden under a tomato bush. I rode my bike over to his house every Saturday morning for the next two weeks to satiate my new appetite.

After two weeks, Scott's mom found the magazine and called my mom and told her. I don't think my parents had a clue, just like most parents these days. They never talked about any of this with me. Instead of punishing me, they turned to James Dobson and made me listen to every tape available from Focus on the Family. I remember listening to those tapes and it only piqued my interest more. What I needed were my parents, not some tapes. Those tapes along with my 1986 Tops Traded Set are currently listed on an eBay auction.

Although I tried every avenue I could to get in contact with it, porn was never really directly in front of me. Porn was an adventure into the taboo, not something I had constant access to whenever I wanted. I worked hard to come by it, just like every other teenage boy I knew, but it's not like I could sit down at the computer when my parents were away and stumble across a sadomasochist website. Nowadays, if kids want porn, they know where to go, and it's as easy as the click of a button.

I made it through college without the internet and a computer, but how are kids today going to go through their cyber-filled lives unscathed? Instead of having to hide a magazine under a tomato bush, kids have access to every fetish and live streaming video. We have to do something.

## THE FACES BEHIND PORN

It's ironic, never having had access to a computer as a kid, that I now spend oodles of time reading and answering letters on the internet. Letters from people like Val.

```
Dear Craig,
    My name is Val and I have been with Eric
for over two years. I believe Eric is my bless-
ing and is to be my husband for life. Shortly
```

after we began our lives together he began his porn addiction. I have tried explaining to him that I am uncomfortable with this and want him to stop. He would lie and try to sneak and erase the evidence but something is always left behind. I brought proof to his attention and he just snapped and punched doors. So then I tried sending him letters and emails; nothing seems to get to him. The last attempt I brought up the pictures he thought he deleted and put them in a folder with a letter explaining the perversion and how I am really hurting over this. I told him that if doesn't stop I would leave. I feel lost and I am screaming in my head at him. I want to be the only one he looks at that way. I feel he is cheating and every person I have talked to just says, "That's what guys do. Accept it."

(Please, I am in need of some heavenly advice.)

I've also received letters from broken people like Al, a fifty-five-year-old man who confessed that internet porn led him to spend four hundred dollars on prostitutes. He had never experienced a problem in the past until he and his wife separated. In 1997, his wife told him that he failed to satisfy her and she divorced him. He would go through several months of not looking at internet porn. During this period he would look for another wife only to find frustration followed by the porn and sex binges. He feels as if God has abandoned him because of his sin.

Bob sent me a letter in which he told me that he wasn't a Christian and didn't believe in my "god" either. However, he went on to write about the necessities of dealing with the "wrongs of porn." Bob knows firsthand because he went to jail because of it. Bob lost his wife, friends, and career because of porn. He writes, "You can't go into porn without getting pictures of younger and younger women. You don't have to have a fetish for eight-year-olds to be labeled a pedophile. If you look at a picture of a seventeen-year-old, one day away from her eighteenth birthday, there is no distinction. You will go to jail, and you will suffer."

Darcy became involved in cyber sex through porn and no one knows her secret. She wrote, "I have two great kids and a great husband but during the day when I am at home by myself I turn on the computer and become anyone I want to be. I don't have anyone to talk to because no one will understand."

A young girl sent me a letter saying she had discovered porn on her brother's computer. Instead of telling her parents, she became fascinated with the material herself.

Veronica, a wife of six months, had her dreams of marriage shattered. She wrote, "I found some disturbing stuff on my hubby's computer from the saved file for instant messenger, stating he wishes he never married me so that he could date again, talking to this girl about nude pictures and seeing her in heels and telling her he will 'do' her all night. I have been crying constantly about this. I feel like he has ripped my heart out."

A man once expressed concern to me for his mom who had phone sex at their house and for his two brothers who looked at porn while at work. He has confronted them and feels that their involvement is tearing their family apart.

Dee is worried about her fourteen-year-old son and writes, "We found out he visited a porn site and has been saying really weird stuff sexually. We have always tried to have an open and honest relationship, where he can feel safe and no question is off limits, but his recent behavior is not cool. Any advice?"

Lisa is another mother worried about her son. She found a porn tape he had made and somehow feels responsible for it. This porn tape showed girls and guys together, girls and girls together, and other graphic sexual images. She writes, "Dear ... Please pray for him. I love him and will do whatever it takes to help him. He seems depressed and so lonely. I just found the tape today, and he wants it back and is calling me terrible names. He said all the kids have porn in their homes."

I sit at my computer and read these letters all day from people, people who struggle with constant online fantasy chatting, people who can't get enough internet porn, people who find themselves less and less satisfied with what they can get easily, so they turn to darker, more extreme material. As I read the letters, I think of the people I know who struggle with this; it helps me put a face to them. But early on in my journey with the XXXchurch, I figured out that I'd have to do a lot more than sit at my computer and read letters to understand pornography. We had to get out among the people consuming pornography and try to put a human face on this issue. That is how Porn Patrol started.

# PORN PATROL 2

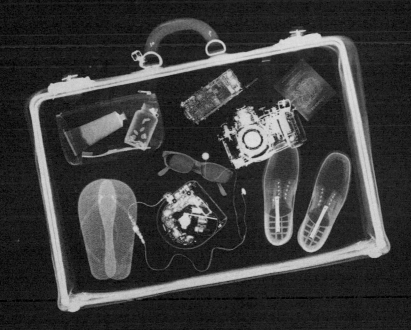

The glass doors of the LA Convention Center stood in front of me for my third consecutive year exhibiting at the Erotica LA Convention. I had arrived early that Friday morning to think about the upcoming weekend. I could still feel my pulse quicken as I stepped into the huge building. I remember the first year vividly. I had no idea what I was doing. Mike and I had just started the XXXchurch and we reserved a booth at the annual convention immediately.

Many people have called me foolish or immature for going. Maybe I am. I am the only Christian pastor to ever pay money for booth space at a convention packed with porn stars, voyeurs, and exhibitionists. People ask me if I've got the wrong convention. "Hey! Church is down the street, man."

We get the same question every year we go, whether it's coming from the media or the church: "Are you making a difference?" And deeply hidden beneath this question lies another: "Are you exposing yourself to porn needlessly?" I can't answer that question honestly and say with a 100 percent certainty that our efforts equal X amount of goodness or affected lives. There have been times when Mike sped away in his truck after a fruitless day at the porn convention yelling, "What the heck are we doing here, Craig?" I have walked away discouraged, kicking myself for not remaining a conventional youth pastor. In fact, after six porn conventions in LA and Las Vegas, I'm still not completely sure what I am doing there. We seriously considered stopping.

Instead, this year we rented two booths. (If you don't quite know the answer, you can always go bigger.) In previous years, we handed out Bibles or cards with the message "Jesus Loves Porn Stars" on them. The first year we parodied the Playboy Bunny and brought our own named Rex the Rabbit, a person—usually one of our wives—inside of a comical bunny suit. The idea was to have an animal character create a friendly atmosphere for porn stars to sit down and talk with us.

This year, Mike and I would be manning the "Porn Challenge" booth, in which we would ask as many customers and proprietors as possible if they were willing to give up porn for seven days. If they could see their lives briefly without porn, would they feel better about themselves or their futures? Three college girls I had met or known as a pastor worked the other booth. They sold and gave away T-shirts with the words "Jesus Loves Porn Stars" on them. Sure, the slogan gets a little laugh, but the real goal was to get porn stars to connect with these girls after the convention and create relationships outside of the porn industry. Critics say we do it only for the press and attention, but we keep going.

The first time we went, we set off a riot of media and press. They showcased us on every news outlet from the *LA Times* to *Playboy* to *Focus on the Family* to CNN to *The 700 Club*. Since that first time, the buzz has died down to nothing. We haven't been on the news for a convention since our debut. Now, three years later, it's just the XXXchurch and the porn industry. I had passed through those doors more times than I can count on my fingers, entering each morning with fresh hopes of opportunity that I might reach somebody. Often I'd leave through that same door in the evenings with frustration or bitterness.

Many tell me that I walk through the gates of Sodom and Gomorrah. They say that the hellfire reserved for this lost flock will devour me along with them. Those who stand outside with megaphones and preach, "All ye who enter here shall be consumed by fire and brimstone," haven't stopped me. I keep going every year. I still pay the union at the Los Angeles and Las Vegas convention centers money to set up my booths.

I realized Erotica LA 2005 was my sixth porn show as I walked into the nearly empty convention lobby. Immediately I saw the banner hanging from the ceiling. One of the girls pictured on the massive piece of canvas, Sara, stood out in contrast to the other four, overpowering them in my mind—not because she was particularly sexier than the other four, but because I knew her.

I walked over to sign up at the registry pavilion in the middle of the lobby, registered my booth, and clipped my exhibitor pass on my shirt. *Here we go again.* I gave one last look at the banner and thought of the two phone calls I had gotten from her in the last week. She wanted out. Maybe we were making a difference.

One thing's for sure: I know the full extent of what I'm up against. I know where the porn industry wants to go and I know that the industry is succeeding. This realization was one of the only true epiphanies I've ever had and it happened just days before this last porn convention at a pre-convention party for the event.

## THE SKY IS THE LIMIT

One week prior to LA Erotica I received a letter in the mail reading "Hottest Party of the Year: Erotic Art and Celebrity Sightings." It was from the Erotic Museum of Art on Hollywood Boulevard. They were hosting an exhibit at the convention for the first time and invited all the exhibitors to attend a party in the museum.

So I left in the Porn Mobile, taking two XXXchurch volunteers, Carter and Laci, with me. Driving into Hollywood I noticed all the grand attractions. I drove past the Mann's Chinese Theater and all the celebrity stars, past the Guinness World of Records Museum, the Hollywood Roosevelt Theater, and many other famous places that attract tourists from around the world. I realized this strip held culture from eras past, over a century of cinema and grandeur.

I wasn't surprised to find out about a museum celebrating sex, the effects of which would be arousal or perhaps an appreciation of beauty. The naked woman is a beautiful thing after all; we have never had to provide an explanation of why men of all ages turn out in droves to the porn conventions. I read the mission statement of the museum before I came: "Our ultimate goal is to provide the community with a positive image of the potential of human sexuality." This might not be so bad after all.

I arrived at the party around eight o'clock and was surprised to see no scantily clad women or pimps decked out in street finery. These were people in dresses and suits, milling around the foyer and looking at art displays. Before I entered, I decided to explore this notion of the "potential for human sexuality."

An open bar sat in one corner, attended by a Chip 'n Dale dancer serving free drinks for all customers. A stairway led to the upper story where the main exhibits were on display, and people in fine clothing came up and down. I got a Coke and stood looking helpless. I took a sip and next to the bar I noticed a stack of cases holding figurines. Some were of men and women in erotic positions but one especially caught my attention, that of a man having intercourse with a goose. *Odd*, I thought.

The upstairs held no guests wielding whips and chains or fat sweaty men in leotards either, just regular folks in suits and ties. One man wore a kilt and marched militantly from display to display, soaking in one piece of art, taking it in, then walking briskly to the next piece.

Instantly, I was overwhelmed by the amount of male genitalia on the walls. The main exhibit held large, human-sized photos on the walls that grabbed my full attention, minimizing every other piece of art in the upstairs gallery. So this was the potential of human sexuality. If sex was space exploration, then I had landed on Mars.

A young man wearing no shirt in a bowtie offered me a chocolate-covered strawberry on a platter. He got this job off of a website. I took a strawberry and pulled him aside, my eyes still on one of the ten massive photos on display. I asked him what he thought of the art.

"I try not to look at the photos. They make me uncomfortable. I'm just here to serve the strawberries, man. I walk around and keep my eyes on my platter."

I looked around at the people in the gallery; everybody faced inward, talking quietly in small groups, away from the art. The young server wasn't the only one. I walked further in the gallery and talked to an older custodian, whose job it was to make sure nobody touched the artwork. We stood under a photo of a woman masturbating a cow.

"The hard thing about it is that I've got to stand and watch this stuff to make sure people don't mess with it. I don't want to look at this stuff, but if that's what you're into then, hey, I'm not judging."

He didn't know I was a pastor; I was just another exhibitor with black earrings from the LA Erotica Convention.

With the exception of the kilt man who stared intently at every piece of artwork, nobody paid much attention. They socialized. Two Asian interns with the press giggled nervously in their pinstripe zoot suits. I asked them about the art.

"Oh, we're not affiliated with the convention," they reassured me. "We're attending as reporters." They looked up at a few of the photos. "We're not into any of the gay stuff, and that," one pointed to the photo directly above them, "just looks extremely painful."

"Have you seen anything that would turn you on?"

"No," they said in unison.

I headed toward the back of the gallery, away from the main exhibit. I passed more people and a large enclosed glass box holding gooey recreations of male and female genitalia. Holes connected to rubber gloves allowed guests to stick their hands through the box to feel and explore the sculptures.

A few guests stuck their hands in but quickly lost interest. Either they were embarrassed to be seen feeling around fake genitalia, or they were beyond getting anything out of feeling the recreated textures; maybe a high school kid might be amused, but not these folks. They were the innovators of sexual exploration, each person bringing something different to the convention. We were told everybody's sexual tastes fall somewhere in between the box with the recreated parts and the photos on the wall, but nobody paid much attention to either. The party was supposed to be a celebration of uninhibited sexuality, but the guests in suits and dresses mostly looked bored and subdued.

I continued back. I felt like Dante, who passed through the abyss in order to acquire epiphany. I still hadn't found my answer to the meaning of the potential of human sexuality. Is there a line to be crossed? In space exploration, nature and time draw a line of where we can go, how fast we can travel, the systems we can see, what planets we can travel to. Did the same rules apply to sex? Did nature—the idea of the "natural," in this case—draw a line to where we should be able to take sexploration?

I stopped at the end, in front of a series of television screens mounted inside the walls. Each screen had something different playing and the date on which it first premiered underneath it. The first screen showed a film from the 1930s, black and white, slightly sped up. A woman on stage, fully clothed, danced around and men clapped fervently—the most innocent thing I had seen since entering the museum. Next was Judy Garland talking to man behind a fence. More movies from the fifties and sixties came next, showing slightly less clothing and more risqué positions, innocent enough.

Then came the 1970s. The first mainstream porn on a screen in succession with the other ones. The screens kept showing the progression throughout the twentieth century. Hardcore porn came on the screens. Things beyond hardcore. Writing on the wall surrounded the screens in artistic script telling about the potential of human sexuality: "The sky is the limit." I looked back at the photos that made everybody uncomfortable. I was looking at the sky. I found my answer.

## EROTICA LA

After attending that party, I decided to pay attention to the progression of this "sexual innovation." What degree of sexuality were these customers going to expose themselves to as they walked through the rows and aisles of the convention? Are we talking missionary positions or bestiality?

To get into Erotica LA, guests have to stand in line. Most of the guests are men. Some are women who came with their boyfriends or husbands. Some of the boyfriends and husbands are bringing their girlfriends or wives into the industry by shopping them around to different companies. Sixty thousand people attend this event over the entire weekend.

I stopped a dark-haired man in jean shorts in line and asked him how long he had been waiting to get in. He said he waited for twenty minutes and still had a while to reach the ticket booth. Once he reached the booth, this man would exchange thirty dollars for his all-day pass. From the ticket booth, he would have to walk up the stairs or take an escalator to get onto the convention floor. Several glass and metal doors separate the large room holding the lobby and stairs from the booths. Once he passes through these doors, he crosses over to a deep red carpet.

The entire affair is set up like a maze; several aisles and rows wind in between company booths. Most booths have only one approachable desk or a small opening where customers can enter and feel like they're in a shop. Others are three-dimensional islands, where customers can approach proprietors from all sides. The arrangement feels random at first impression.

But once through the doors, customers find themselves in a semicircle, the flat half of the circle hugging the entrance wall. There are four or five three-dimensional booths taking up the center of the semicircle. These are the mainstream porn companies, like Vivid and Wicked. They are the most successful and produce porn from the top porn stars and are usually less extreme. From the center, a customer can choose to take any aisle leading outward to the fringes of the semicircle. Clothing companies featuring slogans dealing with sex or porn stay more toward the middle with the larger companies.

The farther a customer gets away from the mainstream booths, the more she is exposed to hardcore material, the smaller booths featuring more violent or intense sexual situations. A parallel can be drawn between starting off with the more mainstream porn, such as the girls with the big names like Sara or Jenna Jameson, where the girls are more respected. However, it's never enough, and the more a user watches or participates the more he or she needs. The porn participant takes a mental journey toward the back of the convention as well as a literal one as porn leads to more porn.

Also, scattered throughout the convention are booths of companies that have nothing to do with porn. Dr. Tanaki, a family chiropractor, has a booth that offers free stress tests and back services. Another company offers nonsexual massages. Liquid Ice sells energy drinks. These companies feel they can make a profit off of porn, and the customers who stroll around are just regular people who need chiropractors too.

I find it amusing that our booths are always located on the very outer fringes. We don't really fit in no matter where they put us — except that once a person gets so involved in porn and finds it no longer satisfies, he or she looks for a way to escape to what really does satisfy.

Immediately in front of the entrance was the "Club Jenna" stage. Every day around two o'clock, Jenna Jameson, the Marilyn Monroe of porn, comes out and signs autographs for a line of people stretching all the way to the back fringe of the semicircle. The line is over a two-hour wait.

Jenna Jameson has rock star status, a porn MVP. A thick semi-circle of guys and girls, ten rows abreast stand below her, calling out her name. "Jenna, over here, Jenna!" They hold cameras over their heads taking pictures of the famed porn queen, snapping picture after picture. So many flashes hit the stage and rebound off the metal railings. So many pictures in so many cameras!

Pictures are what drive this industry, pictures you can get off the internet, in magazines, adult stores, and, if you go to the convention, your very own camera. We had a porn challenge and a message that Jesus loves you, but I felt we needed something more. This year, I wanted to explore beneath the pictures. I wanted to find out who these people actually were, not what their images were supposed to represent. I wanted to get to know the personalities of the people who made the stuff, and I wanted to find out about the people walking the aisles and perusing the porn.

I still show tendencies to judge these people as simple people, individuals who have turned to pleasure to escape their lives. But for all the conventions I've been to, I had never explored beyond my own booth. This year, since I was in the middle of writing this book, Carter and I decided to journey through our surroundings. I had no clear plan except to gain knowledge about the people who worked and attended Erotica LA. I started immediately with a woman standing next to me. She was not what I expected.

Samantha, a lithe woman with dark brown hair, stood in line waiting to get an autograph and a picture with Jenna. Fifteen years prior, she'd written her grad thesis on the Mustang Ranch, a brothel near Las Vegas, and the girls inside. As she waited to meet the greatest porn star of all time, she talked to me about the mindset of the lowly porn star or prostitute, the ones supporting kids and making hardly any money.

Her experience revealed that all of the girls she had been in contact with have been sexually abused, usually by someone within their own family—fathers, mother's boyfriends, uncles. The girls then go into porn because that's what they know. They mistakenly believe that if they're in the business, then at least they have control over it and get paid for it.

As Samantha put it, "The reality of these situations is that they don't have control and they don't get paid. The pimps take all the money. The pimps are horrible, horrible people and they trick them into prostitution. Sometimes they hold them hostage. A lot of times when the girls get pregnant, the pimps steal the babies and get their own mothers to watch the baby. Then the pimps tell the girl that she has to pay him $500 if she wants to see her child again. That's the street end."

"So do you think there's a line with all this stuff? A line of what you should and shouldn't do?" I asked her.

"You know, when I was working with some of these girls, they were talking about priests picking them up and picking up boys as well. This was fifteen years ago and no one believed them. Look what's going on today. Yeah sure, there's a line," said Samantha. "There's a certain type of person drawn to porn, and the number is a lot higher than we think. I had my bag outside the convention earlier and many mainstream girls who look normal ask me what it's all about. They had a real interest. Even if you look at *Cosmopolitan* magazine, there are half-naked women on every single page because people are into it. It's become so mainstream."

"Is there something to be said for a monogamous relationship in today's society, one man and one woman?" I ask.

"Yeah, that's what I have, and I wouldn't have it any other way."

From the Club Jenna booths and other mainstream companies, I made my way toward the fringes, the booths that mostly tailor toward certain fetishes and personal tastes. At one booth stood a bespectacled black man named Troy, who was selling sex toys. I approached him because he stuck out. So far, I hadn't seen anybody else at the convention who looked more out of place than this guy. He had a pleasant smile on his face, hiding what looked to be amusement at his situation. Turns out, Troy was an accountant. He was only selling sex toys that day because the regular salesman called in sick. I talked to him about his real job—internet sales. According to Troy, their product sells mostly from online sales. He thinks people are still embarrassed to walk into a store and buy sexual aids. What's more, 65 to 70 percent of the people who buy their stuff on eBay are women. As Troy puts it, "It's easier to buy online since you're anonymous. There's no face to judge."

"Why do you think there's a certain factor of embarrassment involved?" I asked.

"It's something you don't want your neighbors to know about. Everybody knows everyone's doing it, but you still don't want to put a face to it. That's why you can do it on the internet. The biggest sales on the internet in the beginning were adult sales because people realized that the stuff they wanted to buy was now available without attaching your face to the purchase somewhere," said Troy.

"Is it because they are not satisfied with their husbands or their boyfriends?" I wondered.

"Either there are a lot of lonely women out there or someone's not doing the job," said Troy.

Suddenly, our conversation was interrupted by a loud voice three booths over; "DVDs! Three for ten dollars!" The seller motioned people to stop by his booth. I asked Troy how all the porn around him affected sex toy sales.

Troy claimed that it was a vicious cycle, but in a good way for the industry. "So many of these guys are into porn exclusively that they leave a lot of lonely women behind. We scoop this market of women up and sell them our sex toys." Troy jokes with the guys walking by the booth. He promises them no more lonely nights for the price of twenty-five dollars.

"Do you think there's a line to be crossed, a line where people take porn too far?" I asked.

"Who's to say? If somebody wants to pay for it, then it's going to be done. I may have my line. My line may be way over here, but your line could be way over here."

I left Troy and walked over to another booth, a corral-shaped construct where porn stars sat on elevated platforms and signed autographs. I walked up to Harmony, a porn star. She was signing autographs and posing for pictures with people. A man wearing jeans and a red No Fear tank top waited patiently for her signature.

She signed a large eight-by-ten photo of herself, "To John, love Harmony, XOXOXOXO."

John walked away, reading her writing. A porn star loved him; he could put the picture up on his wall and look at her every night. The reality is that she had already forgotten his face. Why would she want to remember him? Harmony only had two days off of work in the last five weeks filming porn footage.

"Does working every day do anything to your perception of sex?" I asked her.

"No, because I separate the two. For some people it affects them, but I separate the two. It's really easy because the sex is way different from how it is in your normal life. It's not how it seems on the videos. It's work, and we have to be in very awkward positions for guys to see the action. It's not real sex. It's actually like mechanical sex," explained Harmony.

After talking with Harmony, I approached two guys browsing a booth. They were a father and son and both had bags of porn. Their wife and mom thought they were out looking at cars. The son thought that the stuff that happened in the videos was what his marriage bed would be like, including all the hardcore elements.

"What happens if your future wife doesn't want to do some of that?" I asked. He looked confused. He said he would have to adjust.

## PORN CHALLENGE

Most of the day, Mike and I were busy asking people if they could take the porn challenge: to stop looking at porn for seven days and then tell us the results of doing so. We gave the guys who took the challenge free software from Integrity Online. The software acts as an internet filter.

We wanted them to think about it. How deep were they into the material? Were they independent or did porn control them? So many young guys paused when we asked them and thought about the challenge. Then they'd reply, "I can't stop looking at porn, man. Are you crazy?" Was this something they could stop? We asked Bob some of these questions.

Bob was a large white guy wearing a football jersey. He accepted our porn challenge. Bob lingered around the booth and I asked him why he was at the convention. "Where else can you go and see all this? It's what makes America great," said Bob.

"Do you have any ideas about why people are into more of these hardcore fantasies as opposed to normal sex?" I said and pointed toward a booth involving the fetish of cannibalism.

As soon as the word *normal* came out of my mouth, I knew I'd said an archaic word. The word *normal* was no longer accepted here. Bob frowned at the question. "What is normal?"

"Do you have any thoughts about why people would progress to such a stage?" I asked, again referring to the cannibalism booth.

"It's whatever interests them. Everybody's different. This guy here's got tattoos all over himself while some people get a small tattoo. I mean, look at these guys right next to us. How can these guys go around town and pick up a girl off the street and get her to have sex with them in thirty seconds? Some girls get off on that, having sex with a total stranger in the back of a car. You get the ones on film who say okay, and they're making money off of it. It's a win-win situation," said Bob.

"Do you think there's a shady side to porn?"

"There's a shady side to everything. You look around at some of the stuff back over on this side ... those girls in their pictures look like they're stoned out of their minds. They probably don't know what's going on. But it's whatever they're into. It gets them happy. If nobody's hurt, then what's the big deal?" asked Bob. "As long as you are enjoying yourself, then there is no problem. You're not hurting anybody, just like someone who enjoys going to football games; let them go. If you play baseball, then play baseball. To each his own."

I watched Bob walk away and wondered if he would really go seven days without porn. I picked out a short light-haired man in the crowd and shouted, "Sir! Can you go seven days without looking at porn?"

"No way!" he shouted.

An hour later, Brian, a tall man wearing a Harley shirt, timidly approached our booth. He asked me what we represented, so I told him about the challenge. He became interested immediately. The first words out of his mouth were an explanation that he wasn't really into all the porn around him. Brian's car insurance lady brought him to the convention. The woman had always had a thing for him. They were friends, but she was not his type.

"Do you think she brought you here to entice you? Do you think that she's using porn to get you interested in her?" I said.

"Definitely. But honestly, I'm not really into porn. I don't own any DVDs and I don't rent them. Who cares if I like to catch something on the internet for free, if you know what I mean?"

"So do you want to take the porn challenge?"

Brian thought hard for a few seconds and agreed, "I've got nothing to lose." After he assured me that he would really carry the challenge to the finish, Brian took his free software and walked away past the booth next to us on the right.

The booth was part of a family-owned business. They were small, nothing like the fancy Wicked and Vivid booths. The Danes, a husband-and-wife team, approached their girls in a family way. "Come be part of our family. We'll take care of you." The girls, dressed in clothing picked out by the "mom," were attracted to that, especially the girls who had no families. Heather, one of the porn stars selling DVDs at the booth, knows better now. This is her last day working in the porn industry.

Mrs. Dane was Heather's boyfriend's aunt. She told her about their little family business. Initially, Heather said no, but they persisted and she got drunk and comfortable with the people. Six months later, she had filmed seven movies. Now she is jaded but realizes she never wants to work in porn again. Her father is gone, but she's scared her mother and sisters will find out about her work in the porn industry. She just wants to be a pharmaceutical assistant, never to think about porn again.

Is it really her last day? She's selling her own DVDs that make her physically sick to a portly man in white overalls over bare skin. Looking like he spent too much time in a tanning salon, he bought several DVDs already and came to grope her and buy more.

On our left is a company that sells computer technology. They had invented a product that allows customers to pause their movies and take still frame photos from moving footage. Two young men sell the equipment and one of them will end up taking the porn challenge. Customers can watch their favorite films and turn them into photographs. Pictures to blow up and put on their walls. Pictures to keep in their wallets, give to friends. These two guys like many others there never thought they would be at a porn show, but porn has taken them there.

One of the last guys I asked to take the porn challenge was young. He couldn't have been over twenty-one years old.

"No, I won't stop looking at porn!" he told me. "Porn rocks. You can always count on porn. It will never hate you. It will never put you down. It will never make fun of you. It's porn; you gotta love it."

After we had taken hundreds of accepted challenges, our pornographer friend Jimmy D, a short man with shaggy hair and a long beard, stopped by our booth to see how it was going. A year and a half ago, Mike and I were at the Las Vegas Adult Expo. The convention in Las Vegas is the equivalent to Erotica LA, except that the Red Carpet Porn Awards Show event wraps up the convention.

Across from us that year was a hardcore porn movie company. Jimmy D sauntered over to our booth and sat down on our couch. He took his sunglasses off and made sure he was comfortable. He said he enjoyed our website and thought it was great that we were there. We could not say the same to him. We watched in utter discomfort as his hardcore videos played on two large plasma screens the rest of the weekend. By day two we were sick of his videos. A year later we received a confessional email from Jimmy D; it turns out he was disgusted by his own product as well.

The hardest part of the show is that most people are not at a point where porn has hurt them or harmed them in any way or have recognized that this is a problem yet. However, we don't see this as an innocent pastime but rock bottom waiting to happen. They will get there, and from our point of view, the writing is all over their faces. But we have to wait. So we do. We go back show after show, hoping there will be a few who realize they have reached a dead end.

# THE PORN OVER

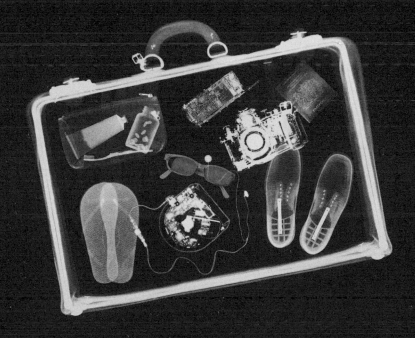

Erotica LA wearied me. I came home after that weekend and just wanted to sleep. I had talked to more people at this last convention than any other I had attended. So many times that weekend I hoped people would tell me what I wanted them to say, or what I think they should have said. I wanted to hear, "Porn is bad … but I can't help it."

I believe that the people I talked to were honest with me for the most part. Where is there a better place to be honest about porn than at a porn convention with a complete stranger who has just asked you to stop looking at porn for seven days? There are no consequences to telling Craig Gross how you feel about the subject and then walking on to the next booth.

I realized how privileged I was to hear people being honest with me. Was there a clairvoyant glimpse of truth among all of this? But then I noticed some discrepancies in the honesty. The father-and-son team I talked to had told the mom that they'd be at a car show. Harmony pretends that she enjoys porn sex.

The worst part about porn addiction is that you can tell a complete stranger what you're dealing with, but you won't say anything to those closest to you. The ones who are most likely to be hurt have no clue, until the addict hits rock bottom. The porn addict lives a lie.

I first became aware that people could even become addicted to porn several years ago. I grew very close to a young man and never knew until much later that he was heavily addicted to porn.

When I was doing my first internship at a local youth ministry in southern California, I met Tim. It was my first Wednesday night at the youth group, and I didn't know anybody—so I went and sat with a couple of seventh-grade guys. Tim was kind of shy. He was the kid most likely used to an empty seat next to him. I developed a friendship with Tim before I got to know anyone else in the junior high group. I tried to bring him out of his shell a little bit. He was really into cars, so we planned a trip to a car show for a weekend. Slowly, he became an active member of the group. Then Tim moved to Michigan with his family at the beginning of ninth grade.

I had no contact with him for over a year until he returned to California for tenth grade. He was a different kid, a whole new person. Something changed him; something got hold of him. He was cocky and arrogant; he changed from a kid who loved cars to something more devious. Every teen goes through awkward phases, but Tim's changes came from sitting in front of his computer, discovering online porn.

During that transition year in Michigan, Tim didn't know anybody. He succumbed to porn through loneliness. He had full access to the internet and he'd look at site after site by himself at night. Suddenly girls were all he could think about. This is the moment that girls became objects to Tim. They hadn't paid much attention to him before, but now he could get all he wanted from any shape, size, and color of girl for free.

Girls stopped being potential relationships for him and became "stupid tricks." Whereas most teens his age would envy finding a girlfriend, Tim started dating girls only to get physical satisfaction.

When Tim moved back to California, his mind was saturated with thoughts and talk of girls. Despite his new obsession, he remained active in the youth group and I hung out with him frequently, meeting together each week for discipleship his junior and senior years. We worked to keep him on the right path. At the time, I was no longer working at the church and had started my own ministry called Fireproof Ministries. We were putting on one-night outreach events for youth and weeklong summer conferences.

Still, I continued meeting with Tim. Maybe I was grooming him to work for me someday in ministry. Maybe I was just concerned about him and thought this was the least I could do for him. Whatever the reasons, I brought Tim with me to Fireproof events and speaking engagements just to hang out and spend time together.

I always thought he was honest with me but later found out he'd never really told me anything. His life was a private morass; he was a stranger to everyone but himself. He wanted to do right but constantly found himself doing what was wrong. That's the problem with porn: it doesn't tell the truth. People caught up in the material don't tell the truth.

I started putting trust in Tim when he had just graduated from high school and didn't quite know what to do with his life. He could have gone to school or got into construction, but he didn't care much for either. He ended up taking the option I suggested to him, which was enrolling in a two-year ministry program for young adults who knew God wanted to use them but didn't want to go right into college. I told Tim that if he completed a year successfully, he could intern with me at Fireproof the following summer.

During his first year at the program, Tim continued his secret addiction. A friend of mine had offered to let Tim stay at her house, and she caught him looking at porn on her computer. He thought he had erased the websites from the computer history, but it seems he didn't do a good enough job. She restricted his computer privileges.

Despite the restricted computer, Tim still needed to fuel his addiction. That was how he found himself outside of a Tower

Records store. He had been there before and knew what he wanted. Tim browsed the aisles, pretending to show an interest in the CDs and books. A balding man with glasses and a beer belly glanced at him from behind the register. Tim wandered toward the magazine aisle. He quickly found what he was looking for—airbrushed girls promised him a good time underneath the plastic wrapping. What did they have to offer him? Tim looked around to make sure no one saw, slipped two magazines in his baggy pants, and sauntered discreetly toward the glass doors.

He felt a hand on the back of his shoulder. "Excuse me," the balding proprietor gestured toward his pants. "Are you going to pay for those?"

"Um ... I'm just looking, thanks," said Tim as he walked back to the stand and replaced the magazines.

"That's what I thought," said the man. "Now get out of here."

Tim had never stolen anything in his life. He never even had the desire to steal anything, but his porn habit had driven him to theft and he had been caught. But that did not stop Tim from returning to Tower Records the following week and actually escaping—this time successfully—with the stolen porno magazines. It wouldn't be the first crime he would commit on account of sex. He finished his first year of the program with lackluster results. Jeff, who headed the program, told Tim that if he finished a summer internship on staff with me at my youth camps, he would let him back the next year.

So Tim went home during the summer, getting ready to work with me. One day, Tim's sister walked into his room to find him looking at porn on his computer with his pants down.

"Ewwww. Gross, Tim; that's disgusting. I'm going to tell Mom about this," she said.

"No, wait. I'll wash your car if you don't tell Mom," protested Tim. She agreed reluctantly. If she'd only known where all the missing ointments in the medicine cabinet went, if she'd been there when Tim used household objects as sex toys, then he would have been washing her car for the entire year.

During this time, and indeed much of his high school period, Tim wasted his life figuring out new ways to please his penis while watching porn. We didn't know how far he had taken things with many of his contact girls, which he referred to as "tricks," since he hid his secret from those of us who cared about him.

Fireproof summer conferences take in five hundred to seven hundred kids from twenty different churches for an entire week. During the junior high week, I felt no need to keep an eye on Tim, but when the high school kids came, I watched Tim like a hawk.

One night, curfew hit at eleven o'clock and many staffers including my wife, myself, and Rick, the camp dean, sat around our condo at the resort talking. We had sent Tim out half an hour earlier to drive down the street to the store for some Ben and Jerry's ice cream. He was a little late, but we didn't seem to notice. Rick went outside for one more check of the resort grounds to make sure no campers had snuck out.

When he hit the parking lot, Rick noticed two people in the white truck Tim was supposed to have taken to get ice cream. Tim was inside with a female camper. It was one thing for two campers to meet up some place after sneaking out of their condos, but for Tim, a staff member, to be messing with an underage girl was outrageous. He could have gotten our entire camp shut down if something had happened.

"Either you can tell Craig yourself, or I will," threatened Rick. Later Tim came up and said he needed to talk to me. What followed was a web of lies inspired by his desire to cover everything up. The events that night led to me shattering Tim's phone, Tim pulling a Dukes-of-Hazard, peeling out at eighty miles an hour, and the end of his internship.

No contact of any form ensued between us for the next twenty-five days. These days of silence for Tim were filled with porn escapades and hooking up with random girls. When we finally talked again, Tim was ready to discuss his problems. The solution I proposed sent him into further denial. I wanted him to go to Porn Prison. Although I did not know everything that Tim was dealing with or everything he had done, between what Jeff and Tim had told me was enough to know he was in trouble. At only twenty years old, Tim could change and put this stuff behind him, but it was going to take some work and some dedication on his part. I could not help him any more, which is why I recommended Porn Prison.

## PORN PRISON

"Hi, my name is Bill and I am an alcoholic." We have all heard of AA and know that the first thing you do is say your name and that you are an alcoholic. Can you be addicted to porn? Can you be a pornaholic? A few months into our journey at XXXchurch we wondered the same thing. We knew the answer was an overwhelming yes, but what does a pornaholic look like and where does one turn for help?

Then we found Porn Prison. Well, that is what we called it. It is a live-in facility called Pure Life Ministries located on a ranch in the heart of Kentucky. The first time I visited, I thought it was going to be a depressing place full of wackos. And it was depressing in the sense of my MTV–Southern–California subconscious, but an atmosphere of hope permeated the entire ranch.

The several acres situated on sweeping forest and grasslands held no temptations closer than ten miles away. That temptation would be the waitresses at the waffle house or girls at the Wal-Mart, a far cry from Huntington Beach. The ministry opens its doors to people who have hit rock bottom. People who have lost it all and have nowhere left to go. People who are looking for help and a way out.

I met several people there who told me their stories. When I met Russell, he had been a resident for six months. Russell's wife left him because of his desire for porn. He loved her but found addiction too hard to overcome. Porn had played a deceptive role in Russell's life. He reached for a need he found overwhelming and only found devastation. Russell was arrested for acting out in a public bathroom.

Images from the very first adult magazine Russell had seen as a kid still haunt his waking moments many mornings. Since his stay, he has been able to focus on what's important in his life. In the stages of his most intense consumption, Russell found the material to be getting more and more progressive. He relied on it more and more because he found it didn't require anything of you as a partner or a real intimate relationship with another person. He found comfort and lived in a blind world. Before he knew it, his world came crashing down and it was too late.

After Russell lost his wife and was arrested, he felt emptier. He turned to porn again for comfort and began to hate it, but he couldn't put it down. That's when he contemplated suicide.

I heard the testimonies of thirty-six guys there who were addicted to porn. Most were eager to talk about the progression of their problem. After returning home I thought, "Could this be Tim?"

Thirty days after the blowout, Tim sat in my living room and I told him he needed to go to Porn Prison. He told me he wasn't addicted. He could stop. He wanted one more chance to prove to me he could stop. I didn't listen to his excuses. He had to go. As I made the phone call to my friend Jack at Pure Life, I begged him to give Tim the next opening, but he wouldn't until he talked with Tim himself. He needed to make sure Tim wanted to be there; otherwise this would not work. Tim left my house angry and bothered that I would recommend this. I asked him if he could imagine what his life would look like in ten years if he didn't go. It might look like Russell's.

Two months later, I sat in Tim's house with his parents and he told me he was going. Once Tim's parents knew the extent of his addiction, they were very supportive. A week later he was in Kentucky.

One month into his stay, Tim stared at a picture frame. His job was staining picture frames, thousands of miles away from Southern California and all the "tricks" on his phone list. Pure Life was going to devote its efforts and resources toward rehabilitating Tim for however long it took.

They never stopped; the wood frames kept coming. He would stain them and more were brought to his worktable. They would be shipped off to Michael's craft stores across the nation and sold to customers for something like $10.99. He would give anything to be back. Back to the beaches of Orange County, riding his bike and staring at the girls that flock to Huntington and Newport with their tanned skin and revealing swimwear. He even missed walking to Trader Joe's to buy groceries. The white wall beyond the sanding and staining machinery gave no solace. It was cold, comfortless.

This was supposed to be the cure for his addictions—his addiction to pornography, masturbation, and premarital sex? Monotonous labor at minimum wage? Most of his roommates and workers alongside of him were fighting addictions to pornography. Some had spent all their money on hookers. Some couldn't get enough phone sex. Pure Life Ministries took all types of sexual addictions and transformed them with their rigorous discipline, heavy Bible studies, ten-hour work days, and the no-talking-to-women policy.

During the first two weeks at work Tim tried everything to overcome the humdrum. He tried to think about God's purpose for his presence at Pure Life, but more often than not, his mind would slip back to the girls he'd had sex with. Or even better, the girls in the pictures, perfect and naked, beckoning from the computer screen and VCR. Sometimes he couldn't control the thoughts; he would excuse himself from the work floot to use the bathroom. Within the locked room, above a dirty toilet, his fantasies would please him. They were perfect women with tanned bodies, and he could make them do whatever he wanted. Tim had never loved a woman. Two minutes was all it took and he was back to staining. The relief would last an hour before the boredom came back.

The heat stifled. Stale air and paint thinner fumes made the work almost unbearable. Tim would arrive at his job at 5:15 a.m., leave at 3:15 p.m., and the work never changed. Radios weren't even allowed.

Over the weeks, Tim kept going to work. He had to. It was part of the program. He began to see some of the grand scheme. They were keeping him so busy that he was too tired to see the naked girls in his mind anymore. He excused himself to the bathroom less and less. He began to look forward to coming to work the more he bonded with his roommates. They kept each other accountable and lived in such close quarters that acting out sexually almost became impossible because of the certainty of getting caught. He began to see that this was a vision of the structure he needed in his life to stay away from porn. Whenever Tim indulged his porn appetite or participated in meaningless sex, his life became chaotic. He came to enjoy the order that Pure Life offered.

Once Tim accepted that he needed to be at Pure Life, he bonded with some of the older guys. They constantly told him that they wished they were in his shoes, learning to deal with the problem while he was young, not having lost everything.

Joaquin bunked across from Tim and woke up with him before work to spend extra time in prayer. He'd been a worship leader at a church in his civilian life. By the time he was caught, Joaquin was so deep into porn and the actions that porn lead to, he didn't even recognize himself. He was forced to confess his sin in front of six hundred people.

One night, Tim and Joaquin sat on the porch talking and breathing the Kentucky air. "I want you to look at your rock bottom point that you never thought you'd reach. I often thought I'd never take it past porn. Those are the things you'll end up doing because porn has such a tight chain on you that the more you indulge in it, the tighter the chain gets and you'll end up doing things you never dreamed you would do," said Joaquin. He never thought he would pay transsexual prostitutes for sex. He did.

Tim listened attentively. "People try to say that porn is great and people try to show couples having a great time with it. The stuff destroyed my relationships with women. The life gets choked right out of you, man. It's a bigger beast than you think," said Joaquin.

Tim also developed a relationship with Ryan, a soft-spoken man sleeping in a room adjacent to Tim's. Ryan is completely bankrupt. He started out with magazines and movies. Then he'd introduce porn to his female sexual partners. He became unable to stop his consumption. Like Joaquin, Ryan's pursuit of porn led him to other things. He began to experiment and poured all of his money into his addiction. When he ran out, Ryan eventually prostituted his body to other men. Ryan found that once he picked up his porn, he wasn't able to set it down or leave it alone. Porn increased to the point that it became unstoppable.

Most of the guys at Pure Life had pictures of their families on their beds to remind them of what they'd have on returning to their lives. Tim had a picture of his parents and older sister. Ryan had the pictures, but his family had disowned him. They won't even speak to him. His friends disowned him too. He didn't realize how much he hurt until he lost people. The pain increased over the last year, when he couldn't talk to his mother. He recalled her voice late at night, telling him how much she hurt inside.

"Now that I've felt the pain I caused her and the rest of my family, it makes me want to change more than anything I can think of. I lost someone I love over something I've done. It hurts not only them but me," Ryan said through tears.

Porn played the major role in losing his family and friends. "They were showing us the phone and said you can call family or friends, and right now there are no friends I would want to call and there is no family for me *to* call."

Wednesday night was Wal-Mart night. Once a week, the guys were allowed to shop at Wal-Mart to buy necessities, toothpaste, underwear, and anything else they needed. Walking down the magazine aisle was prohibited, and there was to be absolutely no conversations with women. If you were seen talking to any girls, your Wal-Mart privileges were suspended.

One Wednesday night, Tim sat out and gazed at the starry sky. Wilderness surrounded him. He had been suspended from Wal-Mart for a month. All the guys were strolling through aisles of civilization. Aisles full of electronics, video games, books, and all the goodies pop culture has to offer. At that moment he wanted to go back to California. How nice it would be to eat fast food again or spend time with his friends and family. Now he couldn't even leave the ranch, except to go to work, and that was the worst part about his stay in Kentucky. A lot of the guys worked with him in the picture frame factory; others worked at the L'oreal shampoo factory. Every job relied on copious amounts of repetition, like staining the same kind of frame over and over or pouring shampoo into bottle after bottle. The monotony taught control, the power to overcome self-indulgence.

His suspension was the new girl's fault at Wal-Mart. She was the first pretty girl he had seen in Kentucky; she tempted him. It wasn't his fault; the counselors made it impossible to even glance at exposed female skin. The trips to Wal-Mart were the only chances he'd ever get. When he learned about the new Wal-Mart girl a few weeks back, Tim put gel in his hair and activated his ladies' man persona. He just wanted to talk to her; nobody would see him. One of his roommates, a middle-aged man named Bruce, wanted to talk to her as well. They sidled off from the group and found her working. Friendly conversation mixed with the suggestive talk that came so easily to Tim took place.

Someone had seen them talking to her and ratted them out. Was it worth it? Brother Brad, the youngest and strictest counselor at Pure Life Ministries, found him later that night and told him of the suspension. "Tim, you're not going to find your wife out here. God has you here for different reasons. Putting him first and serving others is what you need to concentrate on."

Tim set his vision on the starry sky again. He was so lonely—he wanted his friends, he wanted home, he wanted freedom. The porn brought loneliness too, but at least with porn, he was in control. He could look at any picture he wanted and imagine that girl doing wild things to him. Those girls were his—intimate partners to be conjured up and molded to his desires. Here he got in trouble for even speaking to girls.

Tim stopped thinking and looked across the woods and hills. Under the cast of starlight, beautiful trees, and grasses, he breathed the night air. Tears formed at the corners of his eyelids and dripped across his cheeks. He was lonely yet determined. Pure Life Ministries was not a prison; he could leave any time he wanted. God's creation left a calm feeling and he began to realize that God had great things planned for him. This whole thing—his life, Brother Brad, Kentucky, and porn—was greater than himself.

Tim started praying. He wanted God to have control.

## THE ROAD TO RECOVERY?

After a nine-month stint in Porn Prison, Tim was ready to talk. He was tired of hiding. He wanted to be open, not just with me but with several people. When he came back, I met with him every week to talk about what was going on in his life. We'd sit over lunch and talk about our lives. None of the past mattered. We laughed about me shattering his cell phone in the camp parking lot. Tim met with several other friends and church leaders over the next three months.

I believe it was one of the happiest times of his life. Perhaps it was the hardest but he was free—free from the addiction that had robbed him of his future goals and motivation. Tim actually began to formulate real dreams rather than thinking about his dream girl or that dream fantasy. Tim could confide in others and myself and be totally honest about every single temptation or motive.

Two months after Pure Life, I gave Tim an entry-level job doing manual labor at Fireproof events—jobs like filling up inflatable rides and events. Our relationship strengthened as we met together weekly in prayer and went through books. After a while, I took our meetings for granted. I figured that he had been through nine months of sexual addiction camp; he didn't need me as much. I would check up on him periodically and he was fine, cured. I focused my thoughts singularly towards my own life, my family and the XXXchurch.

One night I received a phone call from a friend who leads a high school group at his house. He told me there was a girl in his group who claimed she had been having sex with Tim, before and after Pure Life. Not only did my friend tell me that Tim had been having sex, but doing it in the ministry truck! That's the vehicle that Tim would drive to events and to and from work. I didn't believe him. "Not happening," I said, "I've been meeting with him every week and we are always in conversation." I decided to call Tim as I drove home in the car that evening.

"Tim," I said, "have you been having sex with Amy?"

He paused. "No way, Craig. I'm doing great. I met with you last week and I haven't been having sex with anybody."

I wanted to believe him so bad. He wasn't supposed to get back into it. Pure Life Ministries, those nine secluded months in the Kentucky wilderness, was supposed to cure his sexual behavior. "Don't lie to me, Tim. I got a call from Chris who said you were sleeping with this girl."

He paused even longer. He was trying to hold back tears but they came anyway. "I screwed up again, Craig. I blew it huge," said Tim.

What happened? This conversation rocked my world. Tim confessed that not only was he having sex with this girl, but also he had gotten back into porn more heavily than before. Pure Life had only taught him the right things to say to all of us who were meeting with him. He had learned the language, so to speak. Tim even went out and bought a membership at the local video store, visiting the adult sections every other night.

I sat down when I got home and thought hard. I was sorely disappointed. Could Pure Life not be working? Tim had told me earlier that Bruce, his Pure Life roommate, had recently gone to jail for sleeping with his daughter's seventeen-year-old friend. The man was forty-six years old. Could Tim be on that same path? No, that couldn't be it.

I soon flew out to Kentucky and talked to Russell, the guy who considered suicide as an alternative if he couldn't stay sexually pure. I talked to Ryan, who had prostituted his body for sex and lost all contact with his family. I also talked to Joaquin, the worship leader who had been forced to confess his sin in front of his congregation. Pure Life was working for them.

Then I realized something. Tim has nothing tangible in his own life that can be taken from him. He has nothing that he can physically lose and have a big impact on his life in a real life and death way. Tim keeps going back to porn because he is young. Porn is still a glamorous taboo world for him, and he can sit at his computer in his room and indulge in privacy. The worst external consequence for Tim is his mom walking in on him or me getting steamed when I find out about it. He has learned that it's wrong and he knows people whose lives have been destroyed because of their sexual addictions, but he hasn't really experienced it. He hasn't prostituted his body for sex or claimed bankruptcy because of hookers, like some of his roommates at Pure Life. Tim is still addicted, but he hasn't hit rock bottom.

Things won't always be so consequence-free for Tim. The only current consequences he deals with in his young life are internal as he continues in porn. He feels the emptiness after he acts out. He knows in his heart that it's wrong, but he is in the moment and nothing can stop him. What's going to happen when Tim gets a career? What's going to happen when Tim gets married? Will he be able to shut everything off? Will his wife be able to satisfy him every time in comparison to the range of beautiful naked women he has to choose from on the internet? Forget it. Only then will Tim have something on the line to lose, and he won't know what to do with himself because he hasn't trained his heart or his mind. Most of the time, he gives in to his every sexual fantasy.

I'm often asked, "Are you guys against sex or something? Do you think we should become monks and meditate?" No way. I'm not suggesting that we can just turn off our sex drives, and we shouldn't have to. Imagine life without it. People have to realize the reasons they don't want to be involved in porn in order to get out. Tim doesn't truly realize what he's doing. He may be caught up in the moment, thinking porn doesn't really hurt him right now or not even next week, but he's accumulating a build up, the wedge so to speak. Tim likes to have sex with himself, just as many people do.

This "wedge" of lies and secrecy has the ability to become so powerful that it can destroy the core of a person. People's characters and personalities become a vestige of what they once were or could be, only visible enough to their loved ones and the outside world to hide their secrecy. I fear that Tim could become like Steve.

## THE SPIRAL OF ADDICTION

A man recently sent me his story, but he won't connect it with a name or face, so I'll call him Steve. You see, Steve has a secret. He's addicted to pornography and knows it. The problem is that no one else knows this because he has never told anyone. Steve remembers when he first saw pornography. He was in fifth grade and found his dad's porn stash. He ripped some of the pages out and hid them in his closet. From that day on, Steve was hooked. Sure, besides those few pages Steve didn't see much else for a while. Porn was a lot harder to get back in the days when the only material came through the mail or from the adult bookstore.

Steve watched a few videos and saw a few more magazines by the time he finished high school. Those images were locked in his mind and he could bring them up at any time. Although the exposure to porn was minimal, it was enough to lead to an addiction to masturbation. Once Steve reached college, he got online and things sped up quickly. He could see whatever he wanted to see and did not have to deal with any hidden magazines in his dorm room. None of the embarrassment of getting caught stopped him because he could just erase the history from his computer. Reflecting back, Steve said, "If it was just pornography and masturbation, I think I would be in a lot better shape, but it has progressed to so much more."

Freshman year in college, Steve started visiting strip clubs. Steve is a Christian, but he found himself rapidly participating in dual lifestyles. He would finish up volunteer work at a church or finish a class and then head to a strip club. Sure, Steve had girlfriends in college and could mess around when he wanted, but nothing was like going to one of these strip clubs. He started going and would sit in the back and watch the girls dance. Naked girls, nothing new. Nothing Steve could not see for free online. The difference was that the interaction became real for him. He went because now he could go in the back and actually touch the real life strippers. No longer did he have to sit in front of a computer or masturbate thinking of these images. He could go and get it all for a few bucks at the strip club. Steve always went alone, never bringing anyone to share his experience. He had some friends that would have liked to go, but he could not get past the face-to-face confession, even if it was with peers who would enjoy the experience.

Throughout college, Steve worked at a few churches and kept his problem with porn to himself. He'd disguise himself every time he went to a strip club, wearing hats or trying to hide his face, thinking somebody might recognize him. But the risk wasn't great enough for Steve to stop. Each club held a different thrill for him. Over the years, Steve has visited at least thirty different clubs in several different states. Steve would visit a club every other week, always using his credit card at these places. A cheap lap dance rang a measly ten bucks. Once you try a private lap dance on the beds, the cheap ones cease to satisfy. Those cost Steve anywhere between $30 and $150 dollars.

Every year, Steve found himself sinking further into things that he did not want to get into. He knew the only way out was to tell someone. But he could not and still finds himself unable to. You see, Steve is in ministry. He would lose his job if someone really knew his dirty little secret. Steve has a few close friends whom he has contemplated telling, but he can't ever bring himself to the threshold of revealing his secret to another human face-to-face.

While Steve was engaged to his wife, he made plenty of deals saying, "This is the last time." That never worked. His problems with porn, strip clubs, and sexual fantasies got worse once married. As he puts it, "There is something about this addiction. Sure, we all like looking at naked women. But you are not content to just look after a while, and I can honestly say that this addiction has taken me to places I never thought I would go."

One day while at a strip club, the stripper giving Steve a lap dance offered him a hand job for an extra thirty dollars. He accepted. Up till this point, he had never been touched by a stripper. Leaving the club that day, Steve was in shock. Only thirty bucks. He could only think about when he could return. He wanted more. Steve thought if it was okay to do this at strip club, these things flew in other places. He remembers calling an escort over to the house one night while his roommates were gone.

The week before his wedding, Steve went to his last strip club—or so he promised himself. He could never tell his wife that he looked at porn, revealing his addiction. So he didn't. Ten years have passed and his wife still doesn't have a clue. Sometimes, Steve wishes she would catch him. His activities are getting riskier and riskier.

For about a year, Steve even had Spice TV pumped straight into their bedroom. After his wife fell asleep, he would watch porn and masturbate in bed. Steve describes his sex life as average. Not great, but not bad. He knows how much better it would be if he were not addicted to porn. But porn is easier, so he settles.

Steve could have revealed his secret to his wife at anytime during the last few years, but instead he chose to sink deeper. He's gone to the most dangerous places in the city, driving around looking for places to go. He's blown at least $20,000 on his addiction. He has an arsenal of past memories and images that he can invoke whenever he wishes.

Steve wishes he could tell someone. He wishes he could talk to his wife, but he figures that there's so much potential to hurt her that he would not even know where to start. He wishes he could talk to his friends in ministry. However, Steve affirms that he will never tell anyone any of this face-to-face. He can't, and he knows there are thousands of people just like him hiding their dirty little secrets. So he stays anonymous.

The only way we will ever know his true identity is if he gets caught. Getting caught scares Steve, but obviously not enough because he continues in this. He has installed and uninstalled filters for his computer. Ordered and cancelled the pay channels on cable. Nothing works. Steve thinks that if he could only talk to one person, it would help immensely.

"If I had one person I could confide in, this would all stop tomorrow. I know it because I don't want to do this. I have kids now. I have a ministry, I have people who look up to me, and I feel like they do not know me. Sin has controlled me and it sucks," admits Steve.

So why doesn't Steve tell someone? Fear. Disappointment. Consequences. Failure. And that would mean he would have to stop.

"You will read about this someday, not because I had the courage to finally tell someone, but because I will get caught. No doubt in my mind. I mean that is what I told God to do. And then I will probably have nothing. No wife, no ministry, just more porn. And then will it be worth it? No. But it is not worth it now. Pornography has taken from me, stolen things from me, and cost me $20,000 plus dollars and so much more money can't buy," says Steve.

This story breaks my heart. Can you imagine what Steve would be like if he didn't have his dirty little secret? He'd have the ability to be a great husband and father instead of just giving the impression of being one.

Tim could take the energy he spends in lying to me and everybody else and actually spend it figuring out what he wants to do with his life. But it is so difficult for Steve and Tim to break free because they feel they are alone.

Christians and religious establishments send a cold message to sexual addicts. Sexual addicts are left with the options of accepting their behaviors and facing the emptiness or dealing with being pegged as a freak. From the point of view of a sexual addict, they see only judgment and harsh punishments when confronted with the options of confessing everything and changing. They fear being ostracized — like once they come clean, they need to knock on their neighbors' doors or get up in front of a congregation and admit that they look at porn and be forever branded a sexual deviant.

What has happened to grace? I remember that only God the Father has the right to judge. Can you imagine all of us who call ourselves Christians, walking around this earth with our hearts set on the reality that we are able to give out grace to anyone we come into contact with? Steve would no longer live in fear, hiding from the relationships with his wife and friends that have the potential to save him.

# JESUS LOVES PORN STARS

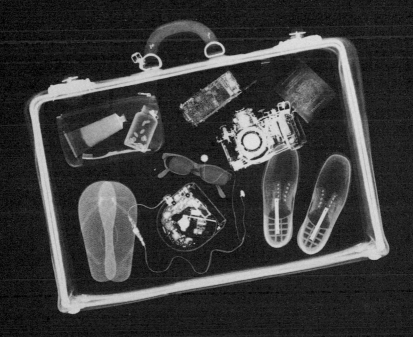

Tim could be our brother. Steve could be our uncle or father. Russell, Ryan, and Joaquin from Pure Life could be close friends in our lives. We care about these guys and want to see them out of their trapped lifestyles. The sexual addict needs grace and support from his or her loved ones, but what about the porn stars? Christians either want to hate them or at least count them among the damned. The rest of the world envies them. These are the women Tim and Steve fantasize about. These are the girls that men choose over their wives.

The song "Us and Them" by Pink Floyd comes to my mind. "Us" being Christians and "Them" the porn stars. To many Christians, they represent the "wayward woman" in Proverbs. I've taken the time to get to know some of these girls, but in my experience, I haven't found any evil Jezebels or vindictive sirens.

Porn star Shauna Grant once said, "All I ever wanted is a house, kids, and a man who loves me." After filming over thirty films, earning over $100,000 in cash and spending most of it on cocaine, Shauna shot herself in the head.

Savannah used her porn star status to date rockers such as Axl, Slash, Greg Allman, and Billy Idol. Men loved her because of her beautiful, innocent face, but she put no effort into her scenes. Male porn stars often compared it to having sex with the dead. At 2:30 a.m., July 11, 1994, Savannah shot a bullet through her head.

Alex Jordan differed from Shauna and Savannah in that she seemed to love her scenes. She would gush that she and her husband had a loving relationship despite having sex with other people in the business. On June 27, 1995, Alex hung herself in her closet while her husband was in Colorado trying to set up a ski shop so they could leave the porn business. A friend of Alex's found her several days later.

Porn star Megan Leigh had just bought her dream house in northern California for $500,000 dollars. One month later, she shot herself in the head.

So often these girls are pictured as rock stars in the media and entertainment industry. Movies glamorize this lifestyle, showing confident people making money doing what they really want to do. They've made it, we tell ourselves. That's what they want to be, and they're happy doing what they want to do.

And then there's Mike and I setting up our booths at the porn conventions. At first we knew nothing about porn stars. We didn't have any porn star contacts. We thought they'd all be Jenna Jamesons, glamorous porn stars with reality TV shows and over-sized bank accounts. We didn't realize that these girls start out at ages eighteen or nineteen looking for the love most of their fathers never gave them, thinking they could somehow fill the emptiness inside by selling themselves.

## HEATHER

Remember Heather, the nineteen-year-old porn star manning a booth at Erotica LA? As a child, she had dreams of being a lawyer, a massage therapist, and a veterinarian. These dreams disappeared when she got into porn.

When Heather initially started, the environment was comfortable and the people were funny. The environment was relaxing for her. She was talked into it. What she saw was a family situation but failed to see its insidious nature.

Heather filmed seven videos from last June to December before she quit, telling her Dane Hardcore "family" she couldn't continue for emotional reasons. Even though she worked at the convention, she was disgusted inside. She was forced to sell her DVDs for a dollar a piece to customers.

She can't believe this is something she ever wanted to do. After her last day, she walked away from it forever. She says she'll never step foot in a place like the porn convention again. "A lot of these girls will say that they like the porn lifestyle, but they're all drugged up when they're on shoots. They're either drinking or they're getting high. So if they can't do porn sober, then why are they doing it?" asks Heather.

Heather used to say she loved it. There was a point in her life where she did love it. "If you don't want anything stable in your life whatsoever, then this is the business for you. I had a lot of fun partying and all that stuff, but I was all messed up. There have been shoots where I don't remember half of what I did. I don't want to be able to say I loved something and having looked back on it, not remembering half of the things I did."

Heather got out while she was young. She can't fathom how girls cope with being in bed with people professionally and still keep a normal married relationship. She identifies least with her porn star friends who are married. "You can't have a serious relationship and do this, because if you really care about someone, you're not going to want them to continue in this. I don't know how some of these girls are married. I'd go crazy." Heather thinks that all these girls really want is love, but they're just in the wrong place. That's all she wanted. Her father left her mother at a young age and she'd never had a father figure step in. She found it at Dane Hardcore, but the experience ruined her.

Heather plans to get a career and start normal life. "Whatever normal is, I want it. I can't be involved with my real family when I do porn. When I'm in the porn lifestyle, I am lying to my family. I'm not going to lie to my mom anymore. If my family knew, it would cause a lot of problems and that's the last thing that I want." Now she's going to school to become a pharmacist's assistant.

She wants to work in the medical field until she is stable enough to take care of foster kids.

## AMBER

Amber is an ex-porn star and a mother. She called me because she had just quit the business for good. For all the work I have done with the girls in the industry, this was the first time a porn star actually sought us out in person, over the phone. I did not quite know what to expect really. Would she be one of those stereotypical girls we see in movies and TV? It turns out that much of her dissatisfaction stemmed from having a daughter and starting a family.

Amber is very close to her thirteen-year-old daughter and began to realize the effects of her legacy shortly before she left the business for good. One day a boy from her daughter's school asked her if he could have a pair of her unwashed panties. Amber knew this boy had been exposed to porn and became extremely uncomfortable at the thought of him talking to her daughter like that. She knows the boys in school are watching porn on the internet, and they talk to her daughter about all kinds of stuff she, the mother, would never even have considered at age thirteen or even twenty.

"As a parent," says Amber, "you know teenagers are going to experiment with their sexuality. As much as I want to protect my daughter, I know she is not a virgin." Amber had made her daughter promise that she would tell her if anything ever happened. One night, a boy Amber's daughter had been dating for eight months had to stay over because of a debilitating ice storm. Amber knows human nature, so she put him on the sofa for the night and stayed on the couch until 3 a.m. before she went to bed.

"I guess something happened. I didn't know until my daughter was late for her period and came to me and said I have to talk to you. She wasn't pregnant, thank God, but it scared us real bad," said Amber. The most disconcerting thing was that the boy talked to her daughter about things and actions only seen in porn films.

Amber sees the progression with how much more extreme porn has gotten and how much it has affected her personal life. "There's some stuff that's just so far out there and kids shouldn't be watching it because boys are going to be expecting this stuff from girls. I don't find this stuff amusing because I don't want my daughter or anybody else's daughter degraded. The stuff they make now makes me sick," explains Amber. "I just think that they figure they have to make it wilder and more bizarre and extreme. There's nothing that isn't out there. They want to push it as far as they can, and there are so many girls willing to do it."

Amber knows girls who have been coerced and set up for a shoot, and when the girl showed up, there were six guys instead of one. The producers will harass these girls, most of them nineteen or twenty years old, if they refuse to continue. "And these young girls are going to do it because they're so insecure about themselves and they let these people take advantage of them," explains Amber.

Amber started out as nervous and insecure as most. She began her career in the adult industry thirteen years ago when her daughter was six weeks old. She was married to a very abusive man at that time. He came home one day and told her that he didn't feel like working anymore. He told her to find a way to take care of their baby. With her baby to feed and bills to pay, Amber did the only thing she could think of. She went to K-Mart and bought a G-string, a bra, and auditioned at the nearest strip club.

Most people get their start in the porn industry via exotic dancing. Amber danced for six months in Florida before she decided to leave her derelict husband. She left for California in 1998. Moving out to San Francisco only provided more opportunities to work in the sex industry. It was here she made her first adult film.

Amber describes that day as the most nervous and terrifying experience she's ever had. At the end of the shoot, she was paid and went home. She started doing more movies because the money was fast and easy. "And then I guess I just got over the nervousness. Once you've been there it doesn't really faze you anymore. You block that part out that says this is wrong or 'I'm better than this.' I fell into an emotional numbness."

During this period Amber married a man who encouraged her to leave everything but couldn't support her. So she continued and worked as a prostitute for a year before a breakdown rendered her emotionally unstable. "I lost it," says Amber, "I was 'out there' mentally. I think a lot of it was the abuse I've been through in this industry and then doing everything I've done."

Then Amber's husband finally found a good job in Georgia and they moved immediately. Her husband started making good money with a salaried job in sales. Amber remembers this year and a half period as some of the happiest times in her life. She started going to church and spent more time with her daughter.

Then 9/11 hit. Amber's husband lost his salary and went strictly to commission. Between the two of them, there was no money to be made. Amber decided she had to pay the bills. She told her husband she would get back into dancing to make a little extra cash. He argued against it but ultimately let her because the bills needed to be paid.

Amber hit the road as a featured entertainer and shortly fell back into escorting and porn. "Once you've done porn," Amber says, "you don't really know anything else, and you're afraid to really try anything else because you don't have the confidence that you are better for anything else. You don't realize that you can do more, and a lot of this revolves around the economic factors."

Amber finally left the business last September. She realized what she was doing now that her daughter grew older and how it would affect her. Amber's daughter knew that her mom was dancing but has yet to find out the extent of her role in the industry.

Amber is now enrolled in school and is enjoying it. She is no longer sexually harassed or exploited. "I'm not totally innocent, but the porn people have influenced my outlook on life and they prey on your emotions and weaknesses," says Amber.

## ADRIENNE

A month before the Erotica LA, porn stars started searching us out. We received a letter from a girl named Adrienne. She was the first porn star I'd talked to who was conflicted with her lifestyle and the Christian faith.

Like many porn stars, Adrienne said and did what people expected and wanted to hear from her. People expected her to be like she was on film, so she acted as if she was having fun with things that caused her spiritual and emotional pain. She'd have to "flip the switch" and be Adrienne, her porn star persona, instead of herself. More and more, she found herself mixing her true self with the person she was forced to play for the camera. As time increased, she found it more painful and difficult to function in the business.

Adrienne's parents had no idea their daughter was a porn star. Her father would often send her letters ending with, "I have no greater joy than to hear that my children walk in truth!" She is pained because she knows how hurt and disappointed he would be. The hardest thing for Adrienne to accept is that someday soon she will have to tell her parents about her life.

She has been a Christian throughout her entire career. "God will not be able to use it for good unless I can share what I have learned from my experiences. And I pray that my testimony will give me a tool to reach out to young people who can relate. I have a long way to go, I know that," said Adrienne.

To make matters worse, she is tormented by her marriage. Adrienne and her husband got into the business together, much like Alex Jordan and her husband. They thought they could make some money for their future and then get out. Now, they are separated and are talking about divorce.

"The hardest thing for me is the fact that our marriage started with God as our Rock. We met through Christians, spent all of our time with Christian friends, and had such a strong commitment to God first. I knew that I was going to marry him two months after I met him. When he proposed, I did not hesitate. And when we said our vows before God, I knew that God had put us together for a reason and that our marriage had God's blessing. It was such a beautiful, Spirit-filled wedding! We said our vows and then celebrated at the altar through praise and worship," describes Adrienne.

Every time she makes up her mind to leave him, she feels convicted, even though he's taken other lovers. He still tells her that he will never give up on her. He tells her that he hates her as much as he loves her. She can't begin to reconcile the image of him at their wedding and his present state of being.

## SHELLY

Shelly has become a friend of mine and our girls who minister to porn actresses. Shelly became a porn star because of her lust for power and her love of money. She never liked sex and was never able to experience sex in the context of a loving relationship. In fact, Shelly was more apt to spend time with Jack Daniels than with some of the male actors she was paid to fake it with. And most of all, Shelly hated being touched by strangers who cared nothing about her.

Because all too often porn stars show up to the set unaware of certain requirements producers place on them, the girls need to perform acts they don't want to do or leave without being paid. Shelly remembers hearing her coworkers vomit in the bathroom between scenes. She chose to cope on the set by smoking an endless chain of Marlboro Lights outside the studio. Shelly admits to having made the choice to put up with the producers as many other porn stars do. But they were manipulated and coerced and even threatened. Some catch HIV from that coercion, and Shelly contracted herpes, an incurable sexually transmitted disease.

Most of Shelly's coworkers admit to experiencing sexual abuse, physical abuse, verbal abuse, and neglect by parents. Some were raped by relatives and molested by neighbors. As Shelly puts it, "When we were little girls, we wanted to play with dollies and be mommies, not have big scary men get on top of us. And we were taught at a young age that sex made us valuable. The same horrible violations we experienced then, we relive as we perform our tricks in front of the camera. And we hate every minute of it. We're traumatized little girls living on antidepressants, drugs, and alcohol, acting out our pain."

But Shelly continued making movies and increased her intake of drugs and alcohol. She lived in constant fear of catching AIDS and other sexually transmitted diseases. Every time an HIV scare hit, she would race to the nearest clinic for an emergency checkup. Due to a no-condom policy (since they obstruct the fantasy), the fear of catching herpes, gonorrhea, syphilis, chlamydia, and other diseases confronted her every day. Even the monthly test Shelly underwent never assuaged her fears. Besides worrying about catching diseases from porn sex, Shelly and the rest of her fellow actresses risked physical tearing and damage to internal body parts.

Shelly's attempts at normal, healthy relationships in her home resulted in boyfriends getting jealous and physically abusing her. Some of her friends married their porn directors while others preferred lesbian relationships. Shelly remembers her lesbian phase. She also remembers having to explain to her daughter why Mommy was kissing another woman when her daughter walked in on her.

On Shelly's worst days, she walked around like a zombie with a beer in one hand and a shot of whiskey in the other. She became too depressed to clean, so she lived in filth most of the time. When she had extra money, she would hire a woman to come in and clean up her mess. Ordering food became normality, after which she would throw up since she was bulimic.

As Shelly reflected on children of porn stars, she writes, "We are the world's worst mothers. We yell and scream and hit our kids for no reason. Most of the time we are intoxicated or high and our four-year-olds are the ones picking us up off the floor. When clients come over for sex, we lock our children in their rooms and tell them to be quiet. I used to give my daughter a beeper and tell her to wait at the park until I was finished."

Shelly is tired of her shameful life and the effects it has on her daughter. She just wants to repair her life.

## PORN STARS

Your average porn star is not a monstrous medusa or harpy; however, she is also not a confident, sexually enlightened individual. She is hurt, broken. She desperately tries to hide it. The large majority of them use drugs and alcohol to escape because they can't handle their reality. They need money and end up having extremely low self-esteem because they compromise their bodies to attain financial survival. They care about their families and how others perceive them. They care about their children.

Heather, Adrienne, and Shelly attest that porn has ruined their love lives. Talking further with Amber, I discovered that she feels porn has ruined a lot more for her. She doesn't believe that porn could even help stimulate people's sex lives as so many claim. Her husband downloaded porn continuously during a time in their marriage. He stopped paying attention to her so she started flirting with another guy openly. Between what Amber was doing and what he was doing, it almost ruined everything.

Amber turned against porn for other reasons too. She has seen damage to our youth and our families, starting with her own life and her daughter's experiences with young guys growing up in the porn generation. She also finds it difficult to see the young girls in the business being taken advantage of since they are the ones who suffer the consequences. When most of these girls wake up, they feel dependent on the business for money, because they don't think they can do anything else. They don't realize that they can do more.

Amber wanted encouragement and someone to boost her self-esteem. She wanted someone to say that she was better than porn. She often looked to the church but only found rejection. Amber currently has post-traumatic stress and a condition called "desensitization and detachment." She can break parts of her personality down to where she's numb to pornography. She can be who she needs to be at that time and be herself later. She is in therapy now because her character has broken into a billion pieces.

Shelly has recently left the business and turned to God to fulfill her broken soul. She writes, "A closer look into the scenes of a porn star's life will show you a movie porn doesn't want you to see. The real truth is we porn actresses want to end the shame and trauma of our lives, but we can't do it alone. We need you men to fight for our freedom and give us back our honor. We need you to hold us in your strong arms while we sob tears over our deep wounds and begin to heal. We want you to throw out our movies and help piece together the shattered fragments of our lives. We need you to pray for us the next fifteen years so God will hear and repair our ruined lives."

Shelly said she felt more comforted by the message "Jesus Loves Porn Stars" than any judgments or calls for atonement for her life choices. Every single porn star we've talked to has said that. They're just looking for love.

Christians forget that these are the people Jesus preferred to spend time with. He shunned or often challenged the self-righteous Pharisees who condemned or persecuted girls like Heather or Amber or Adrienne or Shelly. With his sleeves rolled up, Jesus used both hands to scoop up those stuck in humanity's gutters. In my previous book entitled *The Gutter*, there are several day-to-day examples of how we can go into these places unafraid and unashamed to uplift people in desolate straights. I fear that Christians send a message just the opposite. We appear to the world as moralists, seeking to outdo each other in the piety race. We are a suburbanite, potluck, turn-signaling, Bible-wielding, bumper-sticker group.

We own copies of the *Prayer of Jabez*, which sit neatly by our bedsides. We breed nice guys and gals who'd never be caught spooning or making out in a parked car, let alone associating with porn stars. So many of us go through life without ever getting our hands dirty, waiting to cash in our tickets to heaven and collect our gold stars. The equipment Jesus gave us wasn't harps or clouds; he gave us shovels. Jesus loved the prostitutes and cripples of his day, and he loves the porn stars of today. Where we create stereotypes, Jesus created compassion. He embraces broken girls who've never known the love of a father.

# THE PORN SET

**5**

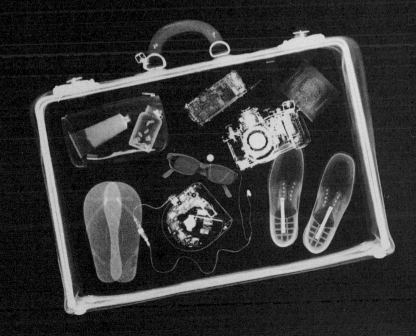

Whathat about the guy who watches porn only sometimes?" I'm asked this question all the time. People feel the need to explain this to me because I am a pastor. "I only watch softcore." "I only go to the websites once every two weeks." The argument comes up that porn in moderation is okay and, in fact, that it can even be good for you. Many compare it to alcohol consumption. Drinking alcohol can be healthy in moderation, and I'm not going to argue that fact. But I will say that porn cannot be done in moderation. I think of an occasional porn habit as little hooks attached by a line to little anchors embedded into the user's mind. The more hooks guys attach to themselves, the further they sink into addiction.

Several days after LA Erotica 2005, I looked at the cards and offers I'd collected in a bag. I picked up a card from the Spearmint Rhino Gentleman's club and their offer for a free piercing. Several more come from hardcore porn sites, offering free rentals or time on their websites. A company that offers phone sex gives you five free minutes. One card from a porn website offers thirty free minutes. The card is firecracker red with a blonde girl giving a seductive look. "Over 10,000 Hot Movies Featuring the Top Porn Stars! No memberships, monthly fees, or credit card required."

What nice guys! They offer a no-strings-attached, half-hour session at their website, and they've got the cream of the porn star crop along with the more personalized fetishes, something for everybody. In reality you get your thirty minutes in heaven but when the thirty minutes are up, you're going to want more.

Most guys would say they'd never pay a dollar to look at porn because they can get it for free. However, you can only get so much for free. These web guys aren't just nice people, and that's why they are giving you three days free. They realize that you're going to want more. That you are going to want the hardcore stuff. You're going to want the full streaming video. You're not going to be content with the sample video that you've worn to death. You know, those twelve seconds of that mpeg. You're going to want the ninety minutes of that uncut version.

That is why so much porn is free. Porn companies just want to hook you in with this bait because once they've got you, they've got the whole thing—hook, line, and sinker. What started out as no membership fees or monthly fees has you breaking out the credit card for more. Why else would a porn site give away free time at their website to browse through all their wares? It's not because they like you or feel you should express your sexuality. They exist for profit. Even after the dot.com bust when many web-sites went bankrupt, porn sites did not. They want to hook you in so you will pay the monthly fee because, let's admit, our brains (especially men) are wired for this stuff.

"The areas that are stimulated by pornography light up in what is called the brain reward pathway. That's where the chemical do-pamine is released when someone experiences pleasure," reads part of an article on Craigslist.com about a man who started out with porn and went to jail for rape; this is the same website from which many of the waiters at the party at the Erotica Museum of Art had gotten their jobs.[1]

This was a letter from a disillusioned young man claiming he'd been ruined, his insides turned to ashes. His secret addiction to internet porn turned him into a closet sex junkie unable to ever see women the way he once did. Who was he? He wasn't the middling couch potato with fading tattoos and playboy cover art splashing across the walls of his run-down suburbia house, somebody's out-cast uncle or tabooed neighbor. He wasn't the party frat-boy with 80 gigs of Jenna and Sylvia and Brianna grinding endless hours of steamy scenes. He wasn't the midnight cowboy traversing seedy theaters in an overcoat, hat, and shades. Not that these types are any more or less susceptible to porn than anybody else, but these are the stereotypes we give them.

He was Mr. Right, or at least that's how he described himself. The nice guy you want to take home to meet your parents; his demeanor includes the following: he is well-dressed, eloquent, and cultured; he opens doors, hails cabs, takes the lead; he is the one nice girls discuss after Sunday church. This darling of society spat vehemence in his letter.

> Do you dream of a man who will love you just for you? Do you believe that you have peripheral, intangible qualities that men of substance will gravitate to? Do you shun the gym in favor of *The Apprentice* and a pint of Ben & Jerry's Chunky Monkey, thinking that your new black pants will sufficiently mask any belly spillage or body expansion? Then forget it. It's game over. You're a walking, talking non-complete clause and you're going to end up alone with a slobbering oversized Rotweiller named Chuckles. Be advised – porn viewing/obsession is spreading like the plague amongst my gender – upping the already unrealistic physical expectations, pushing boundaries in the bedroom (you're down with anal, right?), and providing instant, customize-able sexual highs with the push of a button.

The rest of his advice to twenty-first-century females salivates with sarcasm and hopelessness that reflects on what he's become and the trend he's seen in his age group. This anonymous narcissist advises you to get the boob jobs and the porcelain veneers. Hire the personal trainer. How can most girls match up to the

Jennas, Sylvias, and Briannas? They can't, but they can try their hardest, lest they fear being alone the rest of their lives.

True, this guy is a bit overwhelmingly dramatic, but he speaks from the experience of giving into his sexual desires. He argues that porn has caused his sexuality to take a myopic turn toward irrevocable disaster. He only represents a percentage of good guys you'd like to take home to your parents, right? What's the big deal anyway?

So what if a man's brain is wired for this stuff? Our brains can handle it, right? That's like saying your computer, programmed to channel electricity, can handle a bolt of lightning. But we, in our societal collective voice say, "Give me the 40,000 volts. Shock me, seduce me, pleasure me. I can handle it."

Steve, my anonymous friend, kept saying, "This is the last time." Then the next week would bring another guilty encounter. Then he'd act out with strippers. Then suddenly, porn became the number two evil. Then he would say, "This is the last time I visit a strip club." As time progressed, he developed patterns that made him miserable on the inside, putting all his efforts into a fake exterior.

My cohort, Mike Foster, and I appeared once on Tech TV. Martin, the host, asked us, "So you guys have a problem with people masturbating and looking at porn?"

"Yes, we do," I answered.

"Well, you're married, and I can see how you can say that. For me, I'm single, so this is okay, even two or three times a day, because I'm not married yet," rationalized Martin.

Does Martin think he can stop once he gets married? The patterns that a person is involved in now aren't going to go away because he is married or wants to stop one day. People do not realize that you can't just stop a pattern you've sustained for years and decades because you get married. Many people bring addictions into a relationship or marriage and can never stop.

## THE SLOW DECAY

Jimmy D, my conflicted porn-producer friend, brought these patterns into his life. As noted earlier, Jimmy D films porn. He contacted us and told us he was conflicted with his profession. Fifteen years later he started in the business, and he was only beginning to realize the extent of the damage he had done to his mind. He wishes he could erase memories.

Jimmy D was so conflicted that he offered to direct and film an anti-porn commercial of our choice for free. He wouldn't interfere with the message. He would just shoot. Needless to say, we created a media circus. His colleagues couldn't fathom why he was working with us, and Christians, on the other hand, didn't understand why we would work with a pornographer. We were beginning a friendship.

Jimmy D found himself in the porn business almost by accident. At one point he tried to be a stand-up comic. He toured and did comic shows for three years, trying desperately to make people laugh. He scraped by on meager paychecks. One night Jimmy D lounged at the back of a Hollywood club listening to a comic. She started telling jokes about editing porn and Jimmy D perked up. He had attended film school and knew a lot about editing and film. His dream job was to have a place in mainstream entertainment and he had actually started out as a writer years ago. He wrote an NBC sitcom that never gathered steam and also wrote several film scripts that were considered but never produced.

Once the comic finished her act, Jimmy D approached her in casual conversation about editing porn. She worked as the sole editor for a company called Sin City, and there was way too much work for her to handle by herself, so she asked Jimmy D if he would be interested in making a little extra cash by helping her out. Since he almost never saw substantial money as a comic, Jimmy D agreed. He had never considered getting into the business before, but he needed money.

In three months' time, Jimmy D became head editor for Sin City. He stopped doing the comic act because editing porn for the company required seventy to a hundred hours of work a week. After a few years, Jimmy D had seen vast quantities of porn, and thousands of images were filed in his brain. (He didn't know it yet, but these images would cause him inner turmoil years later —enough turmoil to turn to us pastors, the archnemesis of the porn industry.) Since he was more educated and experienced than most of his peers, he began producing his own porn, and his first project did really well. He made two more installments, which turned out to be one of Sin City's most successful projects.

Jimmy D says his rebellious nature is one reason he was so susceptible to the porn business. Many of his antiauthority sentiments come from his time spent in the Vietnam War. The truth was that Jimmy D was a born rebel. He had been kicked out of the Air Force in Vietnam for protesting the war and writing an underground antiwar pamphlet that had a circulation of ten thousand a month.

So a certain element of the porn business's counterculture persona attracted him. Nowadays though, not only had the bloom fallen off the rose, but it had rotted as a distant memory. If he could make the same amount of money doing something else, Jimmy D would drop the business faster than you could imagine.

Jimmy D has remained smart enough to stay out of performing in his own movies. He's content to stay behind the camera. Male porn stars are often more emotionally unstable than female porn stars. They also get less sympathy because most guys will say, "Why are you complaining? You get to have sex with beautiful women for a living." But even on the other side of the camera, Jimmy D has seen a change in himself: "I think it's inevitable for anyone who works in this business for an extended period of time to have their sexual tastes change. The easiest way to explain it, at least for me, is to say that while my sexual drive hasn't been negatively affected by the business, the things that appeal to me, that turn me on, have been narrowed considerably. They are much more specific and focused."

It's these changes that has made Jimmy D wanted to protect his own children from the world of porn. He is divorced and has two kids: a twenty-one-year-old girl and an eight-year-old boy. Pride comes to Jimmy D's face when he thinks about his son, a brilliant kid. Just last week he said, "Daddy, sometimes I feel like I don't have a brain."

Jimmy D laughed at the time. "Why is that?" he asked.

"Well, sometimes I get to thinking and I wonder that if you and Mommy had never kissed, well, then I wouldn't be here. If I wasn't here ... then ... well ... I wouldn't be here right now to be thinking about it. I can't figure it out ... and that's why I feel like I don't have a brain."

Jimmy D tried to hide his mirth, recalling his own childhood days of thinking about alternate realities and the possibility of the world not existing. He took delight in his own son's innocence, considering his line of work. "Well, if you are thinking about the issue at all, then that means you definitely have a brain," Jimmy D told his son. Great bursts of laughter filled with delight and love for his son echoed for days in his heart.

Jimmy D never lets his son go on the computer unsupervised. He or his ex-wife always monitor the sites he visits and how much time he spends browsing. Knowing the damaging effects of de-sensitization firsthand, he never lets his son experience his life's work. For Jimmy D, kids being able to readily access pornography is a bad thing. Maybe that's why he offered to film our antiporn commercial for free. Well, a major portion of it was for all the publicity to come from our union. He dove into the collaboration, thinking he might get a little money from the deal, but so far he had only gotten grief from the rest of the industry.

Jimmy D can live with the grief, he says, but two years later we now have much more than our kids commercial to talk about. Jimmy D has become a good friend — a guy I pray for almost every day, a guy I would do anything for. I will never forget Jimmy D's daughter introducing Mike and myself to his family and friends at her wedding, which we officiated. He said, "Yes, these guys are pastors, but they are like family."

## LOSS OF INNOCENCE

I remember when Jimmy D jokingly invited me to attend one of his porn sets. I politely declined. But I wasn't the only one he invited, it turns out. Jimmy D invited Carter, my aspiring journalist college buddy, who took him up on the offer.

Carter goes to UC Irvine and is enrolled in the Literary Jour-nalism program. He grew up in Baptist and nondenominational churches, his father often serving on the board as an elder or deacon. Unlike many church parents, however, his mother and father often encouraged Carter to test boundaries. They let him taste their alcoholic drinks or let him watch an occasional R-rated movie at a young age. Carter is twenty-one, stands just over six feet, and only recently had his first serious girlfriend. Little did he know that he would lose something precious forever the day he went to the porn set.

"The opportunity was like none I'd ever been given—the chance to see a real taboo environment, one I'd always been strictly sheltered from growing up," Carter commented to me at a coffee shop several weeks after the experience. "All I needed was an interview with a porn director for my project. So I emailed Jimmy D with the idea of meeting over coffee, and he tells me to meet him at his live set down in the Valley."

So on an early mid-May morning, Carter grabbed a cup of coffee, climbed into his SUV, and realized he was on his way to watch porn stars have sex. Never in a million years had he dreamed of being on the sidelines of a porn set. This experience was supposed to be every college kid's fantasy. They even give out passes to these things on the radio, as if it was a concert or sports game. He was hesitant, however; apprehension set in after ten minutes on the road. Carter's parents raised him in the creed of holding doors open for girls and paying for their dinners. Going to see a woman get ravaged in every way for the camera was not their idea of a healthy sexual environment. But he wouldn't tell them, not like he told all of his friends in hushed excitement. Their reactions varied from, "Don't go; you'll never be the same," to "Sweet! Go and fill me in on all the details."

Carter paused dramatically, searching for words as he continued to relay his experience to me. "Yeah, *conflicted* is the right word. What would my parents think of me going to a porn set? What would God think? But then I just rationalized it in terms of being a journalist because that's what I want to be. You know, an observer."

On that same morning, twenty-one year-old Ariana woke up in the house she owned and headed toward her brand-new Mercedes. The night before, she'd psyched herself for the next day. She mostly preferred to stay inside and read or watch TV, but today she'd earn her paycheck, making what most people make in weeks or even months. As a child, Ariana excelled as a gymnast but gave it up for her current job. Her parents still accepted and supported her, making her a rarity in her profession. Most girls in the industry came from abusive backgrounds or the exotic dancing field.

No, Ariana had chosen to be in this profession of her own will, but sometimes she wondered what her life would have been like if she had chosen a different path. Would she have more friends, be able to sustain normal relationships? Enjoy leaving her house more? She had lost her passion to live life. The fact that she owned the mind of a fifty-year-old man made it hard to have friends her own age. Ariana stepped into her car and drove to Str8Up Studios where she would spend the day feigning submission and having sex with a perfect stranger.

Across town Carter began rationalizing his purpose as he drove up the 405. Was he there to be a "fly on the wall" for his school journalism project, or was he really there for the reasons most college kids would go for? The purpose was the project, but the sex part of the opportunity kept surfacing. The miles slipped away as he approached his destination, Northridge, part of the San Fernando Valley.

Carter sipped his favorite coffee drink, a Starbucks caramel macchiato, and tried to collect his thoughts. "It's like I knew what to expect, people having sex for the camera. Jimmy D even told me I wouldn't be bored. No problem there."

Around 10 a.m. he pulled off on the 101, crossed a few intersections, some old Southern Pacific tracks, until he turned off onto an industrial street taken up by warehouses. Not having seen much porn, Carter wondered what it would do to him. He had seen a couple adult movies with high school friends, and his baseball team had hired a stripper for the shortstop's birthday one summer.

He parked and found Jimmy D waiting for him in the lot. The studio was a beige warehouse next to a tuxedo shop. There weren't any neon lights or billboards advertising its presence. No name on the building, just a metal sheet garage and a side door. The owners kept their business hidden from prying eyes. Jimmy D shook Carter's hand as they walked toward the studio.

"Jimmy D's a cool dude, just a normal guy trying to make a living. We joked around and laughed; I really liked him … I don't think he knew that I came with a negative opinion of the porn industry. He got pretty angry when he found out, as if he had invited a foreign spy to check out his nation's most intimate secrets." A smile broke out on Carter's face as he pictured the angry email from Jimmy D, days after the article Carter wrote came out.

A set hand in an orange shirt loaded backgrounds into a metal bin as Jimmy D and Carter talked about the weather and headed for the door. The mugginess dissipated slightly with help from a few clouds and a soft wind. Swirling through the side door, a breeze ruffled the clothes of two women, a makeup artist, and the freshly arrived porn star.

The makeup artist hovered around the star, Ariana, dabbing blush on her painted face. She was almost ready. The mirror, lit up by lines of exposed bulbs, showed a raven-haired woman, poised to seduce, flaunting her well-defined nose and chin in the reflection. She had dark eyes and chiseled plastic beauty.

Jimmy D introduced Carter to the girls and left to attend to his equipment two rooms over. Ariana rose to greet him. Carter said hello, and she smiled and sat back down to continue the make-up process.

The make-up artist rotated on an axis, looking up in the mirror and back down to Ariana's face. The breeze stopped momentarily and reminded the two of the returning heat of the Valley. The Valley was the porn capital of the world, and Ariana was one of the 1,200 working actors. The industry had just resumed production after a thirty-day quarantine resulting from the infamous HIV breakout. Actor Darrin James contracted the virus on a film shoot in Brazil and brought it back to the Valley. Several actors were infected. It had come as a shock and remained a fear for everyone in the porn business. They were not only afraid of the disease, but that the government might crack down on their no-condom policies. At age twenty-one, what were Ariana's rewards for risking her young life? A great car and a new house.

Jimmy D reentered the room and sat on a stool in the corner. He was a veteran, the old guard of the porn industry. The room was long and narrow with whitewashed walls; a makeup bar and another table with broken chairs lined the walls. Jimmy D wore a blue bandana to keep the sweat from dripping into his eyes. They attempted to keep the room cool; the gentle hum of the air conditioner mixed with the buzz of a large fan two rooms over. Still, his sweat would come; it always did during shoots. Big drops would soak his bandana and drench his blue shirt. The fans would have to be turned off later. A rolling camera in this business commanded silence. Carter stood awkwardly near a metal clothing rack, taking down notes and observing their dialog. They could have been anybody at this point, just regular people.

"How's it coming?" Jimmy D asked. He fired up a Marlboro Light.

The make-up artist, a young woman with perfect teeth, turned. "She's almost ready."

"Good." Smoke curled from his mouth. "For the first shots I was thinking of something colorful. Maybe that orange top?" Jimmy D pointed to Ariana's sprawling mess of clothes spilling from an oversized duffle. "Or something black maybe?" Jimmy D looked to her. "What do you think?"

This was the test. The word "think" wasn't in most of these girls' vocabulary. He usually had to tell them everything. Their sheep eyes blink and their sheep heads nod. Ariana faced Jimmy D and replied, "No black. I like the orange top with the white panties."

Jimmy D smiled; it made work so much easier when the girl could think for herself. He had gone through so many of them. Over the years, this job had turned the female body into a carnal object for him. No longer were they mysterious, sacred, worth respecting. The more you could make them compromise their bodies for the cameras, the more money you'd make, jobs you'd land, and so on. He had seen girls cry while sleazy producers yelled at them to shut up and continue. Most of the girls didn't have a choice; their rent depended on it.

So many guys approached Jimmy D saying, "I'd kill to have your job." He'd smile and humor them but secretly, he wanted to be those guys, back in possession of his youth and second chances. If only he could do it all over again. Carter was one of "those guys," unjaded and still grasping a sense of innocence.

The make-up artist was almost done. Her bag of cosmetics mirrored Ariana's bag. Bottles of cream and powder spilled across the counter. She dabbed one last time; it was done. Ariana was ready. Jimmy D went back into the set room to prepare. She jumped off the stool and dropped her shorts. Carter tried not to stare at the naked girl but couldn't help himself. He forcefully stopped his trembling hands and scratched in his notepad as he asked her a few questions. She talked as a fully clothed human would, while trying on different underwear. Then they moved into the lounge and set room.

It was 11:00 a.m. Jimmy D and Crash, the grip assistant, fumbled through the equipment in the back. Three cases contained over $70,000 of equipment. Jimmy D grabbed his digital camera. It would capture the beautiful tan flesh and processed beauty of Ariana's painted face. He shot a couple tests and peered into the display. "Okay, we're ready for you." Jimmy D waited with the camera and Crash lifted a fill card that would bounce light off of Ariana. "These are just the model shots for the cover of the DVD," Jimmy D explained.

Crash, a balding man only thirty days clean from an addiction to speed, held a fill light up. Jimmy D resumed with the camera. The fan blew cool air on the bodies in the room. "Drop your eyes," Jimmy D directed. Ariana's eyes turned submissive. Her mouth formed a pout.

Jimmy D smiled, "Very artistic. Men are more aroused with a pout than with a smile," he said. Click. Again. Click. Again.

"Porn is art," said Ariana. They laughed at the words and even believed in them. Art has been dangerous throughout history, but only recently have the side effects of art included deadly viruses.

Apart from the aesthetics, Jimmy D had it down to a science. He knew when to zoom in, when to zoom out, when the lighting was working; but most important, he knew the shots that made the money. Deep down, he knew it was the money that mattered, the lifeblood on which his peers sustained their existence.

He snapped a few more shots. "Very sexy when you drop your eyes—very submissive," said Jimmy. She was good. She knew the looks. This was the fun part, the part of the day where they could banter and pretend they were at a casual photo shoot for a fashion magazine. Later, they wouldn't talk so much.

Off camera, Jimmy D and the rest of the crew treated her as a normal person. On camera, however, she's treated no better than an animal, filmed at her peak vulnerability to satiate the fantasies of her customer base.

The digital camera showed submission; men paid money to see her, not artistic footage. Despite her loneliness, she liked the control. She tried to look at life as a glass half full, taking comfort in the sexual freedom.

If she didn't have to make money or buy groceries, Ariana wouldn't leave her house or even drive her new Mercedes. Solitude comforted her. She wanted to think of herself as an optimistic person, full of life. She found comfort in helping people. Just recently she held a door open for an elderly couple going into a restaurant to eat, and they were astonished and grateful. Nobody does those kinds of things anymore. Where'd the kindness in this world go? Many on the outside, Christians in particular, had shown nothing but contempt toward her. If that's all they were willing to see in her—the porn star, and not the real Ariana—then they could choke on their contempt.

Where'd the kindness go? She was kind to the men with the remotes, wasn't she? She helped them with their sex lives. She was all they needed; with her, they didn't have to waste time finding love. They would never have to set themselves up for heartbreak. They would never have to invest their emotions or sit beneath the stars and talk to a woman until the sun rose. While it takes most women a lifetime to reveal themselves, she could do it with the press of a button.

Ariana had a boyfriend, an older guy in his early thirties. He was an adult film actor too, but they didn't have sex. The relationship was mentally monogamous, but they had sex with many other people. Lately he had been getting on her nerves though.

He was too negative, too jaded. He had been in the business too long. She had to think hard to remember the last time they'd had sex; they wouldn't last. She didn't even want sex anymore. It was rare when she had sex off the job or with somebody she knew. Any personal intimacy, special looks shared between two people for instance, vanished as her body washed adrift in the rigors of living the porn star lifestyle, a lifestyle spent mostly in solitude in the confines of her new house.

Despite numerous clichés that porn stars were stupid, Ariana's mind hummed to a bright tune beneath the makeup and powder. She preferred books to television. She enjoyed the escape reading brought. Stories summoned the power to live through the adventures of other characters. Recently she'd devoured *The Da Vinci Code* and was in the middle of *Angels and Demons*.

Often, in her solitude, Ariana wondered about getting old. Whenever she saw a sweet old man, she imagined what kind of man he really was and what kind of life he had lived. Did he have courage and passion? Or was he just another dirty old man beneath the sweet façade, just like every other man she worked with in the industry?

Carter watched her in the back of the room; a few others had gathered for the show, a collection of producers, staff, and actors. "So I had been at the shoot for a few hours and I hadn't seen much of anything. I had pages full of notes about what the people were like and they were all so nice. I didn't get it. Jimmy D laughed all the time and Ariana was eager to share her feelings. Even John West, the bulky porn star, had an easy grin. In fact, when he wasn't on camera, he sat on a couch in the back crunching numbers. Weren't porn stars supposed to be these sleazy, subhuman creatures that exchanged their souls for first-class tickets to hell?"

Carter paused for a moment, recalling the trembling he had experienced on the set. "At first I laughed at all the strange tools and objects they brought out for her to use for these scenes, but then it turned pretty serious. Ariana got so into it … all the screaming and tortured noises, like she was getting raped. She was so different from the person I'd talked to an hour earlier. It was all so violent and she had seemed so nice, almost sweet," he laughed nervously as he talked over his drink, almost trying to make light of the even more explicit images floating through his head, images that will never go away, images that will be with him on his wedding night.

A part of Carter was angered at Ariana and her lifestyle, her new house, and car, and the fact that her mom and grandparents approved of her lifestyle. The other part mourned for her. She would never be able to "make love." It would always be sex, her job. A romantic dinner would be lost on this girl. She is only twenty-one. Carter was the same age and tried to imagine himself in her place.

The footage was halfway through at 5 p.m. The sex had started hours before, but it never lasted more than ten minutes at a time. Jimmy D wanted to go home; it had been a long day. The porn stars resumed, and Jimmy D swooped to the left side of the bed to grab the images and the room grew quiet. Somehow the pleasure of it all was lost in the job. Filming porn deadened him throughout the years. Sexual excitement sunk further away, like a swamp between him and his lost passions. Always abscessing. Always congealing. The latest bridge across the swamp to arousal was bondage images. What would it be next year?

Most of the crazy positions and fetishes showcased in porn are unrealistic and never happen in the real world. If a husband treated his wife half as extreme as the male actors treat the girls on set, she'd have every right to charge him with assault, Jimmy D mused. But the fantasies he had filmed year after year had become his reality. Sometimes he wondered what it would be like to have married one woman and grown old with her. Would he have needed all the bondage, fetish equipment to be sexually aroused by her? Jimmy D didn't think about it too hard; his life was what he made it.

Carter recalled the tension was thicker than the humidity hanging throughout the studio. Not once had the fruition of Darren James and Laura Roxx been mentioned the entire day. Their disease was taboo. Best to forget it happened at all, that it could happen to them. It would be the end of their careers. AIDS could take away Ariana's house and Mercedes Benz, could turn John West's muscles into mush. It had the power to put Jimmy D's son on the street. The industry would shed them like dead cells and grow new ones to continue the exploitation and the fantasies.

"Cut! That's enough. Good stuff, guys." Ariana lay on the bed in a fetal position with her thumb in her mouth. Carter still watched; he had stopped taking notes hours before. There she was, cradled up in a ball sucking her thumb. He'd just witnessed hours of hardcore sex between two perfect strangers. She told him earlier that she enjoyed her lifestyle but this? No, she couldn't. She was only twenty-one.

"I just felt numb all over, just numb," Carter went on. "The feeling grew as I saw more stuff, like bulldozers pushing on a wall until the wall finally collapses. The end result was like getting hit in the face. I knew I'd never be the same ever again."

Ariana didn't move. The producer hugged her, cradling the porn star in her arms. Ariana fell into the embrace, connecting with the other woman, but the producer led her toward John West to film the finale.

Suddenly, Carter felt compelled to leave. "I had to; I just couldn't take it anymore. My legs were shaking so bad. Then I thought that I'd stayed so long I might as well see the whole thing, soak in the entire experience for better or worse." Carter's eyes drift off into space as he talks.

"But I just couldn't; I felt suffocated. I had to leave. So I thanked Jimmy D and said goodbye. I didn't even get to thank Ariana for our conversation. However, I did see John West getting some water on the way out and, well … he was so human about the whole thing. He gave me his number and encouraged me to call him if I had any questions. I could tell he wanted to shake my hand, but didn't. He knew where his hands had been."

Carter almost ran to his car, tired and weary as he was from the exhausting day. During his drive home he broke down in tears. In the coffee shop, several weeks later, it was the part of the experience he felt most uncomfortable talking about. He fumbled for the words, "The tears just came, and like that fact alone can explain it. You'd think I'd have been affected in a different way, you know, every guy's fantasy. That ride home was the saddest I've ever been. The major part of my tears were for what I'd lost. My innocence? I don't know. Something precious, I had gotten a very exclusive view of the porn world at a dear price. I don't think I'd do it over again."

He held no expression on his face. "I also cried for Ariana. She was just so young and my heart went out to her. There's no way she can be satisfied with her life … so sad to me. I haven't cried in years either, not since 9/11. But it just all came out on the trip home, like all the numbness just unraveled into a depression. I was depressed for the next week. Ha, sexual freedom …" Carter laughed insincerely. He was done talking.

Carter left the porn set on that spring day with images of a broken girl, a girl with money and nice things. But at the end of the day, she was still a girl lying in the fetal position sucking her thumb. All thoughts of a horny young girl wanting nothing more than to become his fantasy disappeared. He arrived at his house in numbed silence later that evening. Some of his college friends were over and shouted enthusiastically as he entered the house. He'd told them earlier of his planned adventure and so many of them reacted in open envy. "Come on, take me with you" or "Get me an autograph." Carter wanted nothing more than to go to bed and nurse his wounded innocence.

## DECEIVED

Sexual freedom? Jimmy D, Ariana, and John West are all as sexually free as humanly possible. Carter tasted this so-called freedom for a day; he knows he'd be shattered mentally, spiritually, and bodily if he participated or watched that stuff every day as a job.

Our twenty-first-century lives have become so desensitized that nothing comes as a shock anymore. America has this notion that people like Ariana, Jimmy D, and John West are happy; they have made their lifestyle choices, so don't bother them. That's like telling someone to leave a man sinking in quicksand alone. Whereas heroin destroys the mind and body, porn has the same effect on our psychological and spiritual faculties. The church's answer is three simple words: Don't do it! Yes, but what are you doing to help? The San Fernando Valley says, "Everything is fine, porn should be in everyone's life—why deny your human sexuality?" We all know the results of these empty promises.

In *Brave New World*, a novel by Aldous Huxley, a new world order has created a utopian society where any type of pleasing behavior is accepted and encouraged. In this world, humans are cloned in little modules like in *The Matrix*. There are different caste systems according to societal functions, and all the different groups are happy with their place as a result of programming at birth. The story revolves around the Alpha caste—a beautiful, hedonistic class, all perfect and without awareness of social consequences. The society is futuristic and modern. Slogans like "Everybody belongs to everybody" and "It is every citizen's duty to be promiscuous" dominate.

Indeed, the citizens are just that. They give into their passions and lusts, sleeping with anyone they choose without consequence. Even small children are encouraged to participate in orgy patterns because it is deemed necessary for their future happiness as adults. In order to bypass human emotions such as sadness or emptiness, the citizens in this new order take a hallucinogenic drug called Soma, which replaces the sensations of both alcohol and spirituality at once, without the harmful side effects.

The rest of human society lives inside little bubbles known as reservations; they are known as barbaric and uncouth. They still have mothers, fathers, and monogamy. To the more civilized citizens in the new order, independent and confident with their superior genes and constant happiness, archaic terms such as *family* or even *literature* and *art* are revolting.

The conflict in the story comes from one of these barbarians finding his way into the "brave new world." They humor him to prove that they can be tolerant and accept one so susceptible to emotion in their society. Jon, the barbarian, tries increasingly harder to convince people that there is more to life than one-night stands and Soma. He reads Shakespeare's *Romeo and Juliet* to a classroom of students, and they laugh at his rendition of the story because they cannot understand why someone would kill himself or herself over another human or sadness. They've got Soma to block out their emotions, so they cannot grasp a deeper meaning. Jon eventually dies and everybody continues on with no remorse, only their Soma and pleasure to ward them from the emptiness.

This is the picture often ascribed to the porn industry: a care-free, enlightened atmosphere where people are secure enough in their sexuality to test all boundaries. They are seen as sexual inno-vators and often applauded in certain circles. People are invited to participate in this carefree, hedonistic lifestyle. Any discrepancies, people who show dissatisfaction, are seen as flukes still bound by archaic chains such as the Old World control and the guilt of Christianity and traditional morals. If they only knew what a sham this life really is.

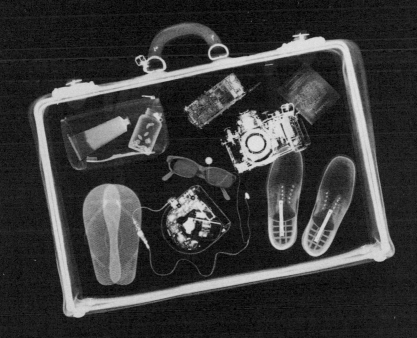

# GROWING UP PORN

Pornography has become a staple of our culture, going ever closer to Huxley's fictional world. No longer is smut the domain of adult bookstores and private theaters. Porn is in your home at the click of a button. It has become mainstream. I met a high school kid in a coffee shop the other day who said, "Porn is everywhere I go now. I can even get it on my iPod and cell phone."

A recent *LA Times* article detailed the scope of its availability. "It's online, on cable, on cell phone cameras, in chat rooms, in instant messages from freaks who go online and trawl children's Web journals, on cam-to-cam Web hookups, on TV screens at parties where teens walk past it as if it were wallpaper, in lectures about abstinence in Sunday school and in health class, in movies, in hip-hop lyrics like the one blaring from the loudspeaker as they line up for pizza and burritos."[2]

Even Gil Reavill, a veteran writer for *Penthouse* and *Maxim*, sees a problem, which he details in his book, *Smut*. Gil never had a problem with society's attempt at making porn mainstream until he had a daughter. "It offends me that so many people who dislike smut are getting it shoved in their faces. This strikes me as a tad undemocratic. No pornographication without representation. It's the cultural equivalent of secondhand smoke. I think adults should be able to use tobacco, just as I am all for adults being able to access sexually explicit material if they want it. But when we get hit with secondhand smoke—or secondhand smut—without being asked, I am offended for myself, I am offended for other people, and I am offended for the children among us."[3]

We are seeing a new generation growing up with the effects of readily accessible porn. Those between the ages of fifteen to twenty-five are the first crop of this generation where porn is like cable TV, but instead of changing the channel, they are given the option of "choose your fetish." A porn star once told me that this age group is most vital to development of what kind of person you will turn out to be for the rest of your life. At the time we were discussing young eighteen- and nineteen-year-old girls who were thinking about joining the business. "If they don't barricade themselves mentally, they'll go crazy or become extremely jaded. They'll spend the rest of their lives looking over their backs waiting for someone to screw them over," said the porn star, as we talked at the convention.

This jadedness and exposure doesn't just exist for porn stars, but for kids with access to computers as well. We meet middle school kids all the time with porn addictions — all because society and even some of their parents say, "This stuff is a healthy outlet for young people."

In just a short time, we've gone from "dropping dime" phone sex and centerfold playboys to sex tapes of Paris and Pamela to bestiality. Our inboxes are full of emails from smut peddlers, and pop-up ads barrage us daily with enticing images. This increase in porn voltage has also put porn in the real world and on the news. Just miles away from my house in Newport Beach, one of the biggest underage sex scandals in the last couple of years has taken place.

Gregory Haidl, son of a police chief, and two of his friends have been on trial for raping an unconscious girl with a pool cue, Snapple bottle, and lit cigarette at a party. Their acts were caught on camera as they were filming their own porn. Their excuse was that the girl had professed dreams of becoming a porn star and they were only helping her realize her dreams.

The *OC Weekly*, a Village Voice publication, has been a major player in crying out against Haidl and his friends' rape video. They even did a front-page article on XXXchurch.com a few years back.

The story has often been a front-page affair for the *Weekly* and nearly every week they've got some type of blurb where Haidl is portrayed as a monster protected by a corrupt city bureaucracy. However, if you turn a few pages past the passionate articles against Haidl and his violent pornographic behavior, you'll find porn. The entire back half of the periodical is made up of pornographic ads and strip club page space. This is how the paper makes its money as they are entirely supported by a sex culture – a sex culture conducive to Haidl's own video.

To Haidl his actions weren't wrong. For most of his young life, he had been exposed to vast quantities of porn. It had become normal to him. He and his friends were only filming a video of a girl who wanted to be a porn star. They had given her alcohol and drugs, but she took them of her own choice.

Gil Reavill got his start in the sex industry working for another Village Voice publication in New York called *Screw*. His descriptions are identical to the *OC Weekly*'s back pages: "I recall very clearly my first exposure to smut, New York style. Like most teenage boys, I had found my way to porn, but in an R-rated sort of way, not an X-rated hardcore way. The first issue of *Screw* I saw that day in 1981 made me feel physically ill. It was not a magazine at all, but a tabloid newspaper with ink that smeared off on the reader's hands. The rag's back pages were filled with ads for prostitutes. *Screw* fulfilled the basic function of a pimp, procuring customers for hookers."[4]

The only difference is that *Screw* was seen as trash and the *OC Weekly* has gained a modicum of local respect and is taken somewhat seriously. I like the paper, in fact. I appreciate the articles, but I have to expose myself to the prostitution ads if I pick up a copy from the newsstand.

Modern culture won't speak out against porn until something like Greg Haidl's incident rears its head. But what's your kid going to do when he's got a girl in his house who wants to be a porn star and happens to pass out. Will he make a video? With porn, anything is possible because of the progression, always needing that stronger hit. A combination of these images with a state of high arousal causes the brain to release chemicals into the system that act as a drug. Like any drug, to maintain the same high, more extreme doses are necessary.

In his book *Porn Generation*, Harvard law student Ben Shapiro writes, "I am a member of a lost generation. We have lost our values. We have lost our faith. And we have lost ourselves. As societal standards and traditional values have declined, and the crassest elements of sexual deviancy and pornography have taken over the public square, it is the youngest Americans who have paid the price. Never in our country's history has a generation been so empowered, so wealthy, so privileged — and yet so empty."[5]

Gregory Haidl was empowered; he was wealthy; he was privileged; and yet, as Shapiro says, very empty. Of course, this problem didn't just begin with the "Porn Generation." We have had a pretty good idea of the beast we face for a very long time.

The pagan Roman poet Virgil wrote a majestic epic called the *Aeneid*. The story follows the survivors of the ruined city of Troy — you know, that awful movie starring Brad Pitt that came out a couple of years ago. The hero of Virgil's story is Aeneas, who salvages whatever remaining Trojan kinsman he can find, shoves them onto what's left of Troy's fleet, and sails off in defeat and despair to start a new colony somewhere in the Mediterranean.

Only then does Aeneas realize, via messages from the gods, that his ragtag group of Trojan refugees are destined for greatness. They are destined to plant Rome, the greatest civilization the world had ever seen. Aeneas sees the vision of Rome's greatness and finds his life's mission.

But of course, a beautiful woman steps in. The Trojans periodically stop at different civilizations for supplies and find themselves at Carthage after a particularly hard stretch of ocean. The ruler of Carthage is a beautiful queen named Dido, who falls in love with Aeneas immediately upon seeing him. In reality, a jealous goddess has poisoned her, but Aeneas falls for her all the same. He ends up staying in Carthage for months as Dido's love toy. Virgil describes them as having an intense passion. Aeneas gives up his sword for fancy robes, and Dido dresses him up in lavish jewels and finery. She turns him into a fancy man, a nancy boy rather than the brave leader destined for greatness.

We are like Aeneas in that we too are destined for greatness, but we can easily sink into the quagmire of sexual isolation. Many of us see greater purpose for our lives but linger in the garden of our sexual passions, content with momentary pleasure as opposed to living the journey.

Aeneas is stuck in the garden of Dido's court before he snaps out of it. He receives a none-too-gentle message from the higher powers and immediately gathers his complacent brood and sails away. He's got the beautiful woman and the bling lifestyle, yet he realizes there's much more. It's hard for us to comprehend because our culture constantly drills the notion into our brains that once we have the girl and the platinum rims on our Bentleys, then we've made it.

Porn does the same thing. It lures us in, posing as the most beautiful, wonderful thing available. We isolate ourselves, enraptured by our new lover; cutting off real, meaningful ties to the people we care most about. Pretty soon, we become like Aeneas and lose sight of our destiny. There'd be no Rome if Aeneas stayed with Dido.

What is it about porn that underneath its flashy exterior is so dark, daunting? Various media sources and advocators of sexual freedoms will often scoff at people who raise this question. "You Puritans! You just want control over our behavior." But look at these denizens of the porn world. Who has any freedom?

We've discovered through fellowshiping with broken souls that porn likens to a cancer of the mind; it takes a part of you that will never come back—your innocence. We've seen so many cases of despair, addiction, and unfulfilled dreams in the past few years that result in failed marriages and even attempted suicides.

Media and the entertainment industry paint this rosy picture of the porn industry every day, saying that we're in the twenty-first century and we can handle anything thrown at us. What they don't tell us are the stories of the countless abused girls on the porn sets or the broken marriages of men and women who have chosen porn. Desensitized humans wrapped up in sexual fantasies, alone in their addictions. Young kids. Kids like Tim, the kid from my youth group. A long time passed before we even knew he had a problem, looking up porn sites and erasing them on the computer history, stealing magazines, sleeping around, and lying to those who cared most about him.

Porn is an addiction rooted in isolation. You feel separated from God, separated from your spouse, separated from your family. You feel like you are in your own dirty little world. As Brandon, a youth pastor put it, "I don't want to feel separated, especially in ministry. What do I have to offer my high school students if I'm off separated into lust and porn?"

I recently came across an article claiming that porn has started to destroy relationships. It was about Renata, a twenty-nine-year-old editor, who broke up with her long-term boyfriend because of porn. As he was spending more and more time online, he began asking her to change her behavior. "He started asking for stuff that didn't make sense to me," she lamented. "There was no foreplay, and I would start seeming prudish if I wanted it."

She personally had no problem getting male attention, but if you're dealing with a girl in a shiny pleather outfit with humongous boobs who's a contortionist, you can't compete. He began requesting special outfits and more oral sex. "It was 'put on these stilettos and dance around.' He would say things that were straight out of a video: 'You do this to me.' It was like having sex with a fourteen year old."

She began to resist his demands, and the sex began to decline drastically, to the point where they were doing it only half a dozen times a year. He would bring his laptop into the bathroom and along with them on vacation. One day, she hacked into his computer and found he had been in a chat room with a woman she knew. She said, "Either it goes or I go." He agreed to put his fixes aside, but three days later she found him on the computer again. Even though he claimed he was working, she could see in the reflection in a window that he was on a porn site. She was stunned he would choose a streaming video over her.[6]

People like Renata's boyfriend develop the idea that what happens in porn is the paramount of healthy sexual relationships. This is another reason why the porn industry isn't supportive of moderation. They're not really selling you simply streaming videos or pictures, they're selling you a lifestyle. They deal in hooks, and they don't let the small fish go free. Every time I sit in front of my TV and watch a beer commercial, the message ends with "Please drink responsibly." Some beer commercials model their entire thirty-second timeframe around someone who denies the very product they're trying to sell at a party because of the fact that they are the designated driver.

There's no such thing as "Please watch porn responsibly." No, they offer you the thirty free minutes and hook to get you back in for more. There's no surgeon general's warning on porn ads on the Web. You don't see disclaimers reading that excessive porn use can cause desensitization and skewed views of healthy sexual relationships. You see words like "Hot virginal sluts" or "Collegiate bares all." Porn is all or nothing and they want everything.

Porn and its proliferation on the internet and in mainstream society have no comparable equal. If we could compare porn with something, then it would be to cigarette smoking or drug use. Whereas cigarettes turn your lungs into black husks, porn gets inside the brain like a parasite.

Some studies even suggest that watching porn changes the physical structures of the brain, compelling users to go back for more like heroin addicts. Sure you're an adult. You can smoke cigarettes and you can watch porn in America. However, if you smoke cigarettes, odds are you will die of lung cancer or heart disease.

Our recent porn revolution starting with the internet hasn't even begun to show the consequences of how they are molding the world around us. The casualties are dying in the slow cooker. They're like the proverbial frog in the pot of boiling water that won't jump out because it doesn't know it's dying. We haven't begun to see the consequences of porn in its new, widespread, eBay, click-of-a-button anonymity. It's the porn that leads to more porn. Most people won't admit they've got a problem until they've hit rock bottom.

Meet Jack, a nineteen-year-old kid from Australia I met in Amsterdam. When we started the XXXchurch, we wanted to get a feel for how skewed sex can get, so we flew across the Atlantic. Welcome to Amsterdam, home to all things pornography leads to. We visited many places, starting with a missions center, but our journey ultimately landed us in front of the red light district downtown—a four-mile strip where sex is legal and pornography abounds. Prostitutes pay a certain amount of money to rent window space so they can attract customers based on their looks and sex appeal.

The night we went, a drunk Jack, vacationing with his friend from Australia, came to check out the hype about the red light district. Jack was a virgin. There to party, none of them had planned engaging in sex with anyone in the red light district. They had come because MTV and other pop culture outlets say that this is the end all of worldly fun places. More important, porn led Jack to believe that this lifestyle brought pleasure. Jack, a typical, good-looking frat boy type, had watched porn on his computer. Now he wanted to be the porn star—to make his fantasies a reality and have no-strings-attached sex with a woman he'd never met before.

"I'm gonna do it," Jack bellowed to his friends, who were trying to talk him out of having sex with a prostitute. He agreed to talk to us after he finished with the prostitute, since there was no way to convince him not to do it. Even his closest friends who partied with him that night had no chance of convincing him otherwise.

Jack went and knocked on one particular girl's door smiling and giving his friends big thumbs up. She opened and he disappeared into her room. Many men walked the strip at this late hour, most alone walking fast with their heads down. They'd knock and disappear just like Jack, but quietly and without the smiles. Ten or fifteen minutes later, whenever they'd finish, these guys would come out the same way, walking fast and looking down at the ground.

They were tourists slipping away from their friends to have sex, or they were veterans of the red light district. Nobody wanted his friends to know, nobody except Jack at this point. Everyone else we tried to interview walked away from us, saying they didn't want to be interviewed, and understandably so.

Fifteen minutes passed and Jack walked out slowly, without a smile. He wanted to leave immediately but realized he had agreed to talk to us. "Ahh mate, it's not how I thought it would be. She wasn't into me; she just wanted to get me out as fast as possible. She was just processing a piece of meat. I was just a McDonald's cheeseburger being processed off the assembly line. I mean, I'm not Brad Pitt, you know."

So many people come to Amsterdam to make themselves a part of the porn. The videos and magazines cease to excite them and they look for new thresholds to cross to achieve the same pleasure.

Proof of this lies down the road, twenty miles outside of Amsterdam and the red light district. The local taxi cab driver who took us to the red light district said, "This is nothing; I'll take you to the real place." It was our last night there, and for only thirty dollars he said he would take us and return us safely.

We drove in a car at about 2 a.m. that February night, negative three degrees outside. We got off the freeway and drove for about a mile. We started to approach a dead end and that's when we saw all of the brake lights. Rows of cars were stopped, waiting in a line. The end of the road turned into a roundabout, a half circle.

Once a particular car's turn came up, the driver would pick up a girl, guy, or transvestite. These prostitutes don't have their papers but still want to sell themselves, so they do it for half the price for what it would cost at the red light district. There were about twenty carports, small little parking spots that you'd find in an apartment complex. Drivers would pull into one with their illegal prostitute of choice and have sex.

I can say that this was one of the darkest places I have ever visited. Condom wrappers littered the ground and the empty faces of the illegal prostitutes of all ages stared out from the cold freezing air. We thought we were at the gates of hell. Cars rocked back and forth. Steamed up windows and silhouettes of bodies going up and down ruled the night.

These drivers weren't people who went there because they simply couldn't afford the red light district. Mercedes Benzes and Jaguars sat right alongside cheaper vehicles. People have money, but they're driving twenty miles outside of town to have some trick for twenty bucks because there are fewer regulations and they have more freedom to pursue particular tastes. They can do more things to these girls because these girls are illegal. Because this porn – the stuff they're hooked on and pay thirty dollars online for a membership – has led to more porn, always pushing boundaries toward the more extreme.

Porn gets you to do things you never thought you could or would do. I'm sure many of those guys in their nice cars with illegal prostitutes never saw themselves ending up like that. A lot of people aren't willing to do anything about it. They see the progression; they see where it's headed, but until they hit the dead end, they wait to turn around. "I can stop looking at porn next year." "I know I'm going wrong way ... but ..." There's always an excuse.

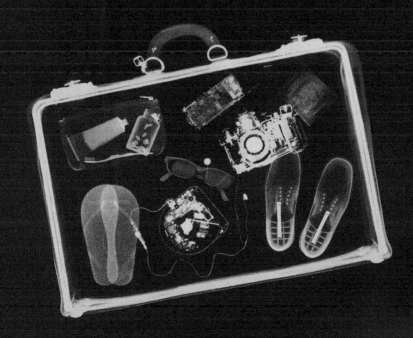

Even though many people are curious about the subject, most people won't talk about it. We have managed to talk about drugs and alcohol, occasionally we touch on premarital sex, but the P word sends everyone running into a hysterical state of denial. Porn is creating wreckage, and it's in the form of you and your family. The stats say you know someone or you are someone who loves it, who can't get enough of it, who stays up late looking at it. Yet we couldn't talk about it if we tried. But we have to talk — and to each other.

Typically men struggle with this, and the best thing that men can do is be honest with each other. One way churches can do this is to have separate groups for men and women, allowing them the opportunity to be honest with each other. It is also a good idea for pastors and leaders to meet to openly share their struggles with one another.

Grand Rapids, Michigan, was bitter cold on January 23, 2005. Mike and I battled weather, airports, and each other, crossing the country to speak at Mars Hill Bible Church. Teaching pastor Rob Bell had a mission: to bring the message of XXXchurch to his congregation of 13,000. It was a natural fit, a progressive message for a progressive church.

Loaded with resources and a documentary film, Mike and I would take over Mars Hill for what Rob called "Porn Sunday." The plan was to speak at all three church services and screen the film about XXXchurch, *Missionary Positions*, Sunday night.

Early Sunday morning behind the scenes it was business as usual for Mike and myself. We said quick hellos and discussed the plan for the service. We were coming off of two years on the road, speaking to Saturday church crowds and at what we called "Porn and Pancakes." This type of event was a great first step for churches to address the issue of pornography, but it was not the best way. Trying to get a group of men to come out on a Saturday morning to church for a breakfast is difficult enough by itself and almost impossible if the discussion is about pornography. A lot of churches seemed shocked when the turnouts were so low for these events, but I came to expect it.

Mars Hill can seat four thousand in the main auditorium. That morning Mike and I began to see the power of a pastor driven to platform a message on a Sunday morning. Rob had been preparing his congregation for weeks and on January 23, it was an answered prayer. People came in droves.

After we spoke at each service, Rob took the stage and told his congregation that he wanted his church to be a place where people could talk about porn. So by calling that particular cold Sunday in January "Porn Sunday," he was sending a message to his congregation that Mars Hill was a safe place to talk about this issue.

That night when over five thousand people showed up to see the documentary, we were all blown away. What was it about this day that brought out so many people and intrigued them? I believe it was the fact that we were going to be addressing an issue that so many members were dealing with.

The next week Mars Hill started several small groups for people who were caught up in pornography. These groups are safe places for these people to continue to go to. The problem did not go away simply because porn was addressed at church. The work has just begun. Our prayer, and I know the prayer of the folks at Mars Hill, is that in the months and years ahead, people will remember what took place on Porn Sunday and remember that it is okay to say the word *porn* at church.

Weeks after the Mars Hill event, steam was building. Churches all over the country wanted to do Porn Sunday at their churches.

Some churches wanted to make a weekend out of it. What happened at Mars Hill spread, and now other churches were ready to follow in their footsteps. Finally churches were addressing the problem of pornography.

We kept pretty busy in the spring of 2005, heading to churches from North Carolina to Canada and holding Porn Sunday and Porn Weekend events. The churches brought us in to talk about porn on Sunday, but come Monday it became their responsibility to deal with it and get people in their churches plugged in and connected with one another. On October 9, 2005, we had over seventy-five churches from around the world take part in a national Porn Sunday. It was incredible to see the church finally exposing America's dirty little secret.

Just recently, I came across a passage in a book by Donald Miller in which he detailed how a woman at a Christian writer's seminar was explaining to him the formula for a successful Christian book. She was telling Donald her theory on what that should be like. First you must start with a crisis—not just any trite problem or annoyance, but a true crisis. She went on to say that your enemy must be clear, in which you, the author, paint yourself in shining white while dousing your nemesis in dirty pitch-black tar. You must show your enemy, whether it is an actual person, government, culture, or philosophy, for example, to be pure evil. From here you must recruit your readers to take an overwhelming stand against whatever it is you are attacking.[7]

Miller is obviously sarcastic about the formula, and I felt a bit guilty. After all, that's what this book is. Am I trying to brainwash my readers? I have an obvious enemy—the porn industry. Do I believe the giant billion-dollar industry is evil? Absolutely. I feel this is a crisis, or else why would Mike and I have started the XXXchurch? I have my brush in hand, tipped in black tar, slathering slick goo whenever I can on what I believe to be evil.

So who am I offending? I guess, first and foremost, I offend the free-speech zealots. I am trampling on the right to expression for anybody and everybody, whether they want to be exposed to the expression or not. Second, I offend many in the church because they believe we've crossed over Acheron and into Hell simply by associating ourselves with this industry.

There will always be critics. Some say that we love the attention, we're not biblically based, we will never see any fruit; some go as far as to protest XXXchurch events. But the bottom line is that we are trying to make it possible to talk about pornography in a country that has wrapped porn addiction up in cute little justified lusts that leads to the destruction of the family. And no, that's not overstating the problem.

I guess we are offending everybody, or at least making them uncomfortable. But that's not what's important. We are sharing what we've found on our endeavor into the darkest possibilities of the human flesh. We see dirty little secrets tearing individuals apart.

I think back to my young friend Tim. He doesn't see the seriousness of what he's doing. You don't know you've hit rock bottom till you actually get there, and that's where he's headed. A lot of these guys are like Tim, who has nothing substantial on the line, and they will eventually find that place where they're broke or utterly, unbearably lonely. But not everybody has nine months to go to a sexual addiction treatment center in Kentucky. Tim was, by far, the least extreme person enrolled.

## PLAN FOR CHANGE

Back in Southern California on a Saturday morning, Vanguard University put together a one-day seminar hosted by Joe Dallas. Joe just released *The Game Plan*, the thirty-day strategy for attaining sexual integrity. Forty people attended that morning to hear what Joe had to say and how people could become clean without having to go to purity boot camp.

Joe is not just some pastor who read a bunch of verses in the Bible and decided to put together a seminar. The man has lived the extreme life. At a young age, a pedophile approached him and introduced Joe to a warped view of sexuality. The man also introduced Joe to some of his friends. He developed a collection of erotica he stored in his tree house and pored over it every day after school. This wrecked Joe, and all throughout high school he was having sex with everyone, including other boys and adult men. It was the 1960s, after all.

Then Joe reversed everything. He found Jesus and touted his new beliefs to anyone whether they wanted to hear them or not. He figured he'd be pure for the rest of his life. He tried to kill his sexuality and often fell into discouragement because no matter how hard he tried, he still lusted, created mental scenarios, and masturbated regularly. He wanted to stop but couldn't.

Practically giving up, his life turned towards chaos again. He spent hours in adult bookstores that led to hookers and fornicating at gay bars. In 1984 Joe had enough. He realized he missed his friends, intimacy with God, and a stable life more than his fantasies. Let's just say the man knows what he's talking about.

After the seminar finished, a young man named Greg stayed behind. He could see his problem developing into a monster that would take the most important things away from him. He'd always said, "I don't have a problem, and besides, I have the right to do whatever I want." He didn't want to go, but Greg's brother wouldn't leave him alone with it so he attended in obligation. Afterward, he thought hard about the issues Joe Dallas exposed.

"My sexual thoughts interfere with my ability to function at work and school. They are more powerful than I am. Sometimes I fail to meet commitments and fail to carry out responsibilities because of my involvement with pornography. I view pornography in order to escape, deny, and numb my feelings. I think about sex more than I would like to," Greg admitted reluctantly.

Greg latched onto the depressing lethality of his life at the seminar. His habits were taking him on a roller coaster ride of fix to fix living. What did the future have for Greg with his newfound insight? Greg stumbled on three key items towards growth and healing:

- knowledge — learning about his sexual patterns
- perspective — acknowledging and creating opinions on the interrelationships causing his dissatisfaction
- motivation — the desire to change

These steps left Greg with a look at what the future could hold for him, but at that point, it would be so easy for him to go home with that knowledge and continue living from fix to fix (one porn masturbation session to the next one). Those three steps meant nothing without the biggest one, the most difficult to accomplish — change. He'd have to actually change his lifestyle. Change is so easy to accept on paper or in theory, but what about when Greg sat in front of his computer with a plethora of beautiful, slutty, nasty, demure girls at his service? What about when the hormones coursed through his system? He would have to decide that he'd rather be free than simply satiated.

Shortly after the seminar, I received an email from Marissa, a woman with questions. Why is this only an issue involving men? When is there going to be a seminar for women? Porn controls my life too. She went on to say:

I spend more money than I can afford to spend on porn. Oftentimes, it seems as though there's a force inside that drives me to pornography and chat rooms. I feel empty and shameful after viewing or masturbating using pornography. One time I swore to myself that I would never again view pornography. It didn't work. I never tell my friends about it. I use porn to deal with, deny, and avoid problems in my life. My sexual behaviors cause me to believe that I don't deserve to have a spiritual life. I have risked losing my job because of my involvement with pornography. I switch channels on my TV and search out sexual content in magazines and books to stimulate me sexually.

## GRACE

My friend Dave sings in a band called PAX217 and now works for the XXXchurch. One night after a long rock show, Dave returned to his house and crashed. That weekend, Dave wished he had nothing to do with his band. He served as a role model to his young fans but didn't feel it at all. He yearned in the worst way to be nowhere else but home. Once in the door, Dave floated past the couch and down the hall that felt about a hundred yards long. He entered his bedroom and immediately fell into bed.

Dave was exhausted. He had no idea how anything had woken him but there was a body hovering over him. Dave felt a kiss on his cheek and then a sweet familiar voice spoke: "Honey." It was Alli, Dave's wife; she had just come home from a Sunday afternoon of shopping and was eager to wake him up. Dave responded by cracking his eyelid slightly just enough to see her. The eyelid went back down, and the bed shifted as she crawled into it. She came close to his ear and asked, "Are you okay?" Dave whispered yes, and then she asked in a softer-than-normal tone, "Can I talk to you about something?"

Suddenly Dave felt nauseous. He had no idea what he was about to hear. He thought for sure she wanted to talk about the horrible fight they'd had the night before Dave left for the show, where he flipped out and yelled at her. All weekend he felt horrible about it. He began to mentally flip through some prefabricated responses, when she asked, "Do you know what I'm going to talk to you about?" Giving her a chance to talk, Dave answered no. She took a deep breath, hesitated slightly, and calmly said the words that Dave never thought he would hear: "I know you've been looking at pornography."

A small painful bolt shot into his mind and he thought, *She wants a divorce ... wait ... no way, she wouldn't leave me.* Then entered his self-deprecating voice in his head, *I blew it last Thursday ... I lost my temper ... she has had it with me.* Looking back, Dave swears his heart paused. Alli hadn't mentioned pornography in a few years. It came up in their first year of marriage when Dave told her that he had been tempted by internet pornography. She cried and made the issue about her, that she no longer satisfied Dave, when in reality, he still thought she was amazing and beautiful.

At that moment, she didn't appear humiliated. Instead, she was clear, and her eyes were full of intent. Dave pictured her mouth opening in slow motion to deliver his sentence; his fear, shame, and pity meters all peeked to record levels. "I know that I have not been a safe person to talk about this with. The last time it came up, I freaked out. But I want you to know that I understand, and I would love to talk about it with you," said Alli.

At first, Dave thought she was playing a twisted joke where he thinks he's forgiven and then she picks a choice moment in the future to open the file cabinet of his bad choices and slaughter him. Dave wanted to back out of the conversation immediately. How could he openly talk about porn with his wife after he had been caught? At the very worst, would he be looking for shelter for the night at the park across the street? Dave knew he had been busted. His dirty little secret was out. Allison, the person his actions affected the most and who would be hurt the most, knew.

Dave chose to talk to Alli about everything and now has no regrets. He gave her his trust, and she gave him God's grace. She went on to say how that weekend she had an intuitive feeling that he had been looking at pornography. On Friday morning she woke to the thought, *Pornography. He's looking at pornography, that's why he was so mad on Thursday night.*

Alli explained how she had seen his rage for the first time from an outside perspective, like she was outside of the room and could see him angry with himself. It was the first time for her that she had not thought that his anger was because of her and directed at her. She was devastated by his actions at first. Through some different ways, God showed her that the act of looking at porn was not about her and what she lacked as a woman, but it was about Dave's issues with intimacy. They went on to talk about how lonely he felt and how when he looked at porn Dave isolated himself from her, his best friend.

"To be absolutely honest, I chose to have sex with myself and the fantasy of women on the internet rather than with my wife. We talked about fantasy; about how when life doesn't meet my expectations, I look for a place to retreat. We realized together that fantasy is lonely. She told me about her fantasies and I confessed

mine. She knew all my dirty secrets. I explained to her what looking at pornography was like—the way it felt to be trapped by the
temptation, falling into it, completing the job, and feeling the wave
of guilt crash down like a tsunami," reflected Dave.

She listened as he told her what it felt like for days after the
fight, and he asked forgiveness for lashing out against her because of his anger toward himself. They sat on the bed for about
four hours that Sunday afternoon, talking, crying, and getting
everything out in the open again. Dave had a best friend again,
someone who knew him completely and loved him anyway.

When this couple's own personal Porn Sunday took place, Alli
and Dave were one week away from their four-year anniversary.
Their marriage was good and they loved each other, but something was off. Dave felt that he did not have the freedom to tell
Allison what was really going on. In a lot of ways they didn't connect like they did when they were first together, and Dave kept his
true feelings away from her because he couldn't handle her disappointment. They lacked honesty and true intimacy, and although
Dave's definition of intimacy was and still is a little unclear, he
knew there was more.

Dave needed and wanted affirmation from his wife. When
Dave's desire for validation outweighed his desire for truth and
honesty, he found himself feeling unknown, reserved, and walled
off. He couldn't help but think that if she really knew him, she
wouldn't love him. Their connection, before they laid their inner
selves out on the bed that Sunday, was like actors in a low budget
'70s film, a repeating scene that could make anyone sick. They
were the two lovers running toward each other on the beach, with
the sun on their faces, a perfect breeze, a sparkling ocean in the
background, and the camera focused on their sappy expressions.

They would finally meet, embracing one another on the "nauseous shore of love."

You know the scene that I'm talking about, right? Well, the thing about that scene is that it took them a long time to actually connect and embrace each other. What the camera didn't show in the film were all the "outtakes." They would run toward each other but would end up about twenty feet apart, like two opposing magnets.

Dave and Alli longed for deep intimacy, but somehow kept missing each other. There were times Dave felt hopeless; they had repeated the same pattern many times and he had ended up in a rotten, self-defeating, nonloving world of porn. Alli, however, had remembered this core part of love called grace. She loved Dave beyond his selfishness, beyond his fantasy world of porn, and deeper than his surface level wall of intimacy. Grace and love never fail. As you give them to someone else, you also experience them. Porn Sunday was as powerful for Alli as it was for Dave; she experienced raw, God-given compassion, and was able to listen like never before. It's bizarre and wonderful, but I think it is easier to accept grace more than other material things because with grace you don't feel as though you owe the person. It's a gift from God: "I choose to love you and I am doing so regardless of your bad choices."

I don't think Dave really knew grace until that day. Grace erases the insatiable desire to judge others. Dave reminds himself what freedom he now has and how much porn controlled him in the past. He connects with his good friend Ryan and me on a regular basis about his sexuality and we hold nothing back. Talking about porn and telling their stories keep them from it. They have exposed it, and Dave has no desire to tell a different story.

Grace is contagious. I have seen it spread all over Dave and Allison's life; it is the translation of God's love. As humans we seem to be pretty consistent at making mistakes, don't we? We all are like Dave and have a need for this grace. We need infinite love, mercy, and favor, shown by God. And when we show it to each other, God imparts it to us.

What is it that we have not been willing to tell for fear of judgment? Have we ever truly known grace? Are we willing to put ourselves out there and trust God for grace? Are we willing to trust others for grace? Dave can, and this act has made his life more fulfilling than it ever was.

Our stories might not be like Dave's, but it could be. Have we, like Alli, chosen to give grace to those around us, placing no judgment when they thought we would? Loving them no matter what?

## ACCOUNTABILITY

My friend Brandon is a high school youth pastor at a church in Los Angeles. While he was studying at college, he became addicted to porn briefly. One day Brandon said, "This has got to end," and he did so. However, like my young friend Tim, he would slip back into porn every once in a while. His usage of adult material wasn't enough to be a debilitating problem, but he still came away with guilt and emptiness after indulging his temptations.

After he landed his first a job as a junior high youth pastor in Anaheim, Brandon would abstain from porn for weeks or months at a time. Then after some time, he would become discouraged with work or his dating life and revert back to looking at porn in the secrecy of his home.

Unexpectedly, Brandon got a phone call from his coworker, the high school youth leader. He told Brandon that the church had fired him. They had caught this coworker looking at porn. Brandon was shocked; his friend was distraught. He had become frustrated with the ministry and looked at porn for a week on the church computers before getting caught by the elders.

The church immediately put out a statement that there would be no tolerance of porn at all. Brandon put some of his past behaviors into perspective. He realized his job was on the line; he could lose everything. Rather than indulging his sexual life behind his friends' and family's back, Brandon chose to stop completely. He looked at what he had to lose and decided porn wasn't worth it.

Church isn't the only place where people are losing their jobs over porn. Most companies have a termination policy for employees who actively pursue porn on work computers. In a web usage survey published by Websense, a provider of employee internet management software, 22 percent of male employees and 12 percent of female employees admit to having visited a porn site at work.

Brandon got married five months ago. Still, he has to be in constant conversation about his temptations. He feels almost as if he's part of a "pornographers anonymous" group, having that awkward conversation with a couple guys he's really close to. Even when Brandon sees a girl in a coffee shop or on the street, he will tell his close friends whether or not she's lingering in his thoughts. Sure, we might say that's a little trivial, but Brandon loves his wife and would rather focus all his sexual energy on her rather than some girl in a bikini on the beach. You know the maxim that guys think about sex every seven seconds on average. Brandon wants to channel those constant thoughts to his wife as she plays a huge part in his recovery. She tells her husband, "I want to be your fantasy. How can we make this work?" Both claim to have much more fulfilling relationships.

Brandon puts it in perspective: "My marriage could end in a second. Ministry for me could end in a second. My high school pastor started getting really discouraged with the ministry, and I don't think he really had an outlet for that discouragement. He had about a week of looking at porn and he'd never really been into it before. But the elders caught him and fired him. And I was working directly under him and I've definitely had times in my life where I've looked at porn and for me this was a huge wake-up call."

Because Brandon is open with his wife about his struggles, getting married has helped him a lot in the past few months. His wife knows how easy this stuff is for him. She realizes how susceptible to temptation he can become. Brandon sits with her at night and talks to her. He reveals that there are thoughts waiting to overcome him. Just being able to share those things in honesty with her makes them that much closer. She's not thinking, "You don't love me." Brandon lets her understand what it means to be a man and makes himself vulnerable. He remains in constant conversation with her because he can share his weaknesses. They have freedom in their honesty.

Brandon talks of his experience with porn as a separation, isolation, lack of community. As humans, we long for connection. And so one of the best ways we have seen people deal with this issue is how Brandon and his wife are getting through it—with accountability. Accountability in its simplest form is having a good friend stick with you in tough times. There are times when people make mistakes. Usually they are alone. What makes porn so damaging is because of the internet, it can be done in complete privacy, with no one around. Accountability is enlisting a friend to come along your side and help steer your direction when you may not be strong enough to resist temptation.

At XXXchurch we have created accountability in software called X3watch. You can download this for free from XXXchurch. com. Place a friend's email address in the program and then every fourteen or thirty days, an email lets the friend know of every website you have visited in the last month. When you know someone will see that you have gone to a porn site, most people think twice before doing so. But it has to be a friend with similar beliefs about porn and someone who will be willing to call if something shows up on the site that is inappropriate.

To me, X3watch is not just about porn, it's about community and accountability. My wife and my best friend receive my accountability reports. I don't worry that they will find porn on my reports. However, I know at least twice a month I will have two people who are looking out for me and will ask me the tough questions.

This accountability should also be found in our churches. Small groups are great if you can go a little deeper and open up to one another. If you lead a small group or are in a small group, maybe you can connect with just one or two people in that group and start holding each other accountable.

Maybe you are not in a small group. That does not mean you can't be accountable to one another. My best friend and I live four hundred miles apart. We don't meet weekly and only see each other a few times a month at the most. But we both are honest and open with each other and realize the value in our friendship and being accountable to one another.

When I say *accountable,* I mean something more intimate than the word applies. The root of the word means "to count," and if that is all we are doing—counting each other's mistakes—then the healing process will go nowhere. We have to truly care about ourselves and our friends for this to work.

Brandon and Dave stress the importance of finding a teammate, a lab partner with whom you can experiment with which techniques work and which don't. It's really hard to keep that focus, but finding a few of those close people that you can really be open with frees the secrecy. Not just an accountability partner. I thought I was acting as Tim's accountability partner, but I was really just having him recite memorized "Christianese," language that sounds holy and fulfilling. I realize now that most of it was faked.

To be at our full potential, we need people in our lives that go beyond saying, "Let's be accountable to one another." We need someone who commits themselves to the battle. Someone who says, "I don't want to be dependent on this either ... this sucks!" You have to want it badly. Otherwise, you are like an ex-smoker who doesn't buy the pack but bums cigarettes off anybody and everybody. Newsflash! You're still a smoker.

Once you get to the point of exposing your deepest sexual psyche to close friends, those conversations will be like exposing the darkness. Just by talking about it, like, "I'll see you later ... Are you going to go home and look at porn and masturbate?" Inside, you'll be thinking, *Okay, my friend just asked me if I'm going to go jerk off right now.* But when you get home still thinking about those words, you're most likely not going to want to do it anymore. Talk about dulling everything down.

One of my favorite movie scenes is in the first Austin Powers movie. Austin sneaks into Dr. Evil's lair only to bump into three incredibly hot fembots, mechanical girls with machine guns in their breasts. Their mission is distraction. They surround Austin and seduce him even though he needs to save the world from Dr. Evil's machinations. They are like Odysseus' sirens, beckoning him toward destruction. Austin starts to shout, "Margaret Thatcher naked on a cold day! Margaret Thatcher naked on a cold day!"

He's invoking a very nonsexual image to overcome his own sexual desires. Odysseus had his sailors fill their ears with wax and tie him to the stern so they wouldn't be lured. There are preparations we can take to overcome temptation.

## LOVING PEOPLE

One way to help our friends is to be someone they can look up to. Be a King David. Be an Aeneas. Sure, these guys stumbled like all of us. Look at King David. This warrior king, a man after God's own heart, committed adultery with Bathsheba and then murdered her husband so he could have her. Next, he tried to cover the whole event up.

But God showed King David grace. The nation of Israel showed him grace as well. If this broken monarch could end up as the forefather of the line into which Jesus was eventually born and one of the great heroes of the Bible, we can see through example that God can make wondrous and strong things from weak, human material. So how can we Christians condemn or abandon those of our brothers whom God himself wants to rebuild and use for greatness? Our struggling boyfriends, husbands, fathers, mothers, children, and pastors are much more than just Christians ripped untimely from the path of righteousness. They are great reservoirs of strength that can only see fulfillment with our support and grace.

As Christians we need to be more accepting and less judgmental. Many Christians see porn stars as pure evil, people gone over to the dark side, exempt of all morality. They are marked for death; they are beyond saving, taking sides with darkness.

I would like to give you the secret to fighting porn. You don't have to make picket signs or boycott the internet. Don't tell porn stars they're going to hell. They have had enough nasty experiences dealing with people who have done that, and doing so will only make them more bitter against Christians and the faith. Understandably, most people in the industry have had really bad experiences with Christians to begin with.

You can also try to go the hard route, which is creating some type of institution or scheme to overthrow the entire industry. Recently, I read an article from a conservative writer saying that we've lost the war against porn. His solution: tax them to death. You can try something like this, but let's face it: with the rapid communication technology available, porn will never go away. Try telling a thirteen-billion-dollar-a-year industry to get up and walk away.

The real battle starts inside the individual. It starts with you. Not what you can do, but who you are. The first thing we can do is simply talk about it, get the skeletons out of the closet, and put them out on the living room couches. Only then can we truly address them, whether it's you or your family or friends.

God is not dead to this issue; he created us this way as sexual humans, but he didn't create us to live in secrecy and fear. The fear only gets in the way of our relationships with Christ and those in our circles. This is not an easy road. In fact, it's downright hard, like the longest road in Africa, a potholed stretch of broken dirt and asphalt running through the waterless deserts of Ethiopia and Kenya where armed bandits known as *shifta* shoot at and rob travelers for their shoes.

Along this road will be a lot of prayer and study. There will be pain like you've never felt, and there is danger. Yes, Christ can take the weight of sexual sin, but we must talk about it and get accountable. Teddy Roosevelt once said, "Far better it is to dare mighty things, to win glorious triumphs, even though checkered by failure, than to take rank with those poor spirits who neither enjoy much nor suffer much, because they live in the gray twilight that knows not victory nor defeat."

I am one of the Porn Pastors. It's a title I don't know if I like, but it's a title I'm stuck with. Every day I hear a story about how porn has made its way into someone's life. The problem is large, and it's just going to get larger. But the issue should no longer remain a secret in our churches. We have groups for drug addicts and alcoholics, but porn and sexual addiction remains the dirty little secret amongst our congregations. The sooner we change that, the sooner our enemy will weaken. Let's dare mighty things even if we fail or find ourselves robbed of our shoes along the way. That's a much better alternative to hunkering down behind judgments, fears, denial, and secrecies.

# PORN AGAIN

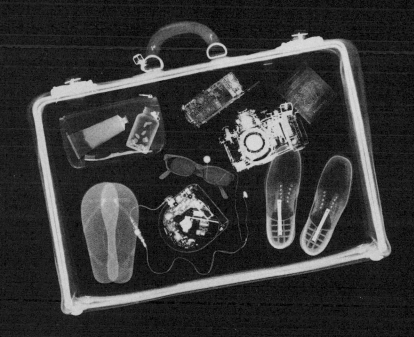

Back at LA Erotica, I ran into two women of a feminist bent, taking interviews from people standing in line waiting to get into the convention. They were filming a documentary on the subject and they interviewed me. They asked various questions about what the XXXchurch did and what people on the inside were like. At the very end of their interview they pointed to the line of men of every age flowing out the convention doors and into the street and asked me what the answer was. They wanted a formula, an equation. They told me I would make a lot of money if I could find this magical answer—the answer to every man's sexual hurts, the answer to depravity, the answer to filling the bottomless hole that men fill with porn but continue to be hungry. The truth is, there is no xyz equation.

Brandon, my youth pastor friend, thinks Christ allows us to struggle so we can fight and press on, so we won't be complacent. It's not like anyone can say, "I've got everything figured out, and I'll never get into this again." The truth is, the consequences are still there in the life after porn. Christ gives us grace, but this thing will never be over; we are still susceptible. It's not as if any of us can move out in the forest in a cabin to get away from it, and I'm not saying we should since that's a form of isolation as well.

Brandon knows a guy through high school ministry who struggled with homosexuality. He never really broke free. This kid, only sixteen at the time, would act out with older men. He'd have intercourse with these guys more because he wanted to be held at the end of the day than anything else; he just had this need for intimacy. It's such a sad story, but he compromised his sanity for moments of intimacy he so desperately craved.

Some people choose a really difficult road; if this kid ever really wants to get back on track, he's going to need counseling. We need to develop more leaders who are capable of doing this and are aware that kids like this are not freaks and that they are capable of healing.

I'm so encouraged by my youth pastor friend Chris because he's doing the right thing and he works with kids in the heart of Vegas. Chris has shared openly with several people about his struggles with pornography and how it had a strong grip on his life.

What's encouraging for Chris is hearing other church leaders (i.e., elders or other pastors) who come out with their struggles with pornography. Many pastors deal with porn constantly, attending conventions where movies are always accessible in hotel rooms. For them to share their stories allows some guy who's struggling himself to say, "Wait a minute: I'm not alone in this. Here's a guy who's a leader at a church and he's struggling."

Skip and Stacy are also doing something to fight porn. A couple months ago, these two guys from Jackson, Mississippi, offered to fly me out and talk to me at their office. Back in the tech stock craze of the late '90s, Skip and Stacy owned several dot.com companies. Right before the crash, they bought a small company called Integrity Online. The company offered filtered internet for people who wanted to protect their families and themselves from unwanted solicitations from porn or other advertising.

These guys were worth millions. Only months before they were about to sell all their companies and retire, the market crashed. They lost almost everything, everything except Integrity Online, which had depreciated in value drastically. They held onto the small company and nursed it back to health. These devout Christian men, in the heart of the Bible Belt, found their very existence depending on whether people wanted to fight the problem of porn. Like Mike and me, who felt God's calling, Skip and Stacy trusted God in this cause completely. They put their livelihoods, their families, and their reputations in the hands of Integrity Online.

I admire Skip and Stacy. Over a meal of fried catfish and pot o' greens, Skip casually remarked that he was going to the Baptist Convention of America uninvited to set up a booth. He would create a stir until people saw the need to confront this issue or he got kicked out. This sounds more like the tactics of a 1960s' hippie than a Christian conservative in the heart of Mississippi. Stacy has the same fire, whether he's battling porn or getting kicked out of his son's Little League game for arguing a call with the umpire.

These guys have let all their reservations go. They are open, honest, and committed. They attest that God has put them in a place where they need to fight to survive. Skip drew me a mental picture during my trip from Robert Lewis's *The Church of Irresistable Influence*[8]: "Christians are on an island and the rest of humanity lives on the mainland. A bridge connects the two groups. Both parties are shouting to the other one, 'Come over to us!' 'No, you come over to us!' And nobody moves. Then we say, 'We'll meet you half-way.' That's not good enough. We Christians need to go all the way across the bridge. We need to get out of our churches and into the gutter, or else nothing will get done and the stereotypes about Christians will remain the same."

Skip and Stacy understand while so many others remain clueless as their friends and family live with secrecy. It's a sad thing, but the people who understand best are the people on the inside of the industry. They're not caricatures of hedonism. They are people who get it, but they get it at an overwhelming cost to themselves, their boundaries, and their sanity.

## BREAKING FREE

My friend Josh, an insider in the porn industry and also a Christian, illustrates how difficult it is to break free from porn. Josh tried almost exclusively to get out by himself. He had all the right signs. He had the motivation to get out, but there was always that something getting in the way of freedom, and it takes others to see that roadblock for what it is. Unfortunately, I didn't see it until it was almost too late.

At 4:30 a.m. on December 29, 2004, Josh slipped in and out of consciousness. He grasped on to the sound of rain spattering the metal shell surrounding him. A headache pounded his skull; he must have been out for thirty seconds. His seat belt felt more constricting than it should have. He wondered if he was bleeding. He didn't feel hurt. He felt gravity trying to drop him unnaturally onto his passenger window.

He checked his face and body for signs of blood. Nothing. His new white Toyota Tacoma rested on its side, facing the downpour on the outside lane of the freeway. Wetness covered his face through the opened passenger window. He looked around for his camera equipment; it was gone. It must have flown out of the window, sitting in a puddle somewhere. Hopefully, he could still salvage the expensive camera and the irreplaceable tape inside. Still dazed, Josh looked out of his tilted windshield to watch semi after semi run over seven signed red DVDs strewn over the pavement.

Thirty minutes earlier, he headed south on the Interstate 5 freeway toward San Diego. His mind wandered as he drove. At 3:50 a.m., the rain crashed down on his windshield. So many things entered and exited his head that he couldn't concentrate. Josh worried mostly. Anxiety about money, or his lack of it, consumed him. He was on the verge of claiming bankruptcy. His car payments were too much, and the rest of his bills were running out of control. Try as he might, Josh could never hold onto his money.

Maybe he should have thought more before venturing out on his own. He wanted to be making fast money so he could start several business ideas he had developed over the years. Josh chose internet website design and video editing as his profession. He loved it; the work made him happy. He enjoyed creating, and his parents always told him as a kid that he would change lives. His mom especially encouraged him to dream big.

Josh glanced away from the freeway heading to his left. A brand new digital Sony camera rested on the passenger seat. The sleek object felt good in his hand. He loved the feel and weight of the piece, the smooth click of the snapshot, the steady recording system, everything about it. He tried not to think of how much it had cost him or how much he couldn't afford it. He tried not to think of what he used it for. The thoughts attacked him, a constant barrage of dollar signs and credit debt. He'd have to rely on his current venture to get out of debt.

Josh felt the clean sensation of the hundred-dollar bills in his pocket. They didn't feel as good as they should have. Guilt rolled over him as he thought of the work he had done that rainy night.

Suddenly, the tires slipped, riding on a puddle instead of the asphalt. Josh's nerves tensed. He let off the gas a little and his tires reconnected with the pavement.

He needed to pay more attention to the road, but his mind kept slipping. Josh started thinking about God. He remembered becoming a Christian years ago; the message he had received at a San Diego church seemed meant just for him. His friend Andrew stayed and prayed with him. Andrew kept Josh's budding faith alive for the next couple years until he moved to Arizona.

Then Josh forgot; the money overwhelmed him. He'd always had trouble trusting that somebody else could solve his problems, even God. He wanted to do mainstream video editing for Hollywood, but wasn't good enough since he hadn't gone to school or received training. So Josh started getting into porn. He figured that his skills were compatible with the Old West mentality of the industry. You were only as good as your drive and persistence in the porn business. Talent didn't count for everything, after all, it was just sex. No complicated graphics or lighting, the business was formulaic. People wanted to see sex and as long as they got good lighting and decent performances, they were happy.

So Josh started attending "Porn Star Karaoke," an event at a Los Angeles bar where porn stars party. He built up solid contacts and landed occasional jobs. Josh started getting to know everybody in the business, learning how to operate in this world. Sometimes as he looked at his future, it depressed him. He didn't know if he wanted porn editing as a career. He decided to do it just until he got enough money to start a legitimate business. On the side, Josh tried his hand at filming videos for churches. Despite his work in the porn industry, he still felt a strong connection to God.

Josh always carried two business cards: one black and one white. The white card advertised a Christian-based, one-man media company. He'd shoot and edit church videos, promising quality work dubbed over with some uplifting Christian songs. He'd landed this kind of work, but usually churches asked him to do it for free. Their unspoken rhetoric: "You're doing Jesus' work and he would want you to do it for free. Think of it as accumulating another treasure in heaven."

Working for free never put any food on his table. It didn't help with his looming bankruptcy problems either. True, the work he got from the white card was more fulfilling, but the black card jobs paid a lot more. Whenever a potential customer gave Josh a call and said they'd gotten his card, he'd ask what color card they had. He didn't want his customers knowing about the other side.

Several days earlier, a well-known porn star needed to refurbish her website. She called Josh from the black card he had given her at a porn convention. He drove up to LA from his home in San Diego and picked up some photo and film work from her to turn into a website. He also took a few glamour shot pictures of her.

The camera he loved so much held her still frames, pictures he would put on her website the next day. The money in his pocket would only make a small dent in his credit debt though. The most overwhelming obstacle in his life was money, and it had driven him to do things he didn't necessarily feel good about. His truck payment was due at the end of the month and Josh had no idea where the money would come from. Sometimes Josh prayed that God would show him a way to take care of his financial problems. He prayed that he didn't have to stay in the porn business for too long.

Before Josh knew what happened, his tires hydroplaned again. This time his control wavered. He let off the gas and tried to remain calm. But the truck spun around and careened off the embankment to the right of the freeway. The truck finally rested on its side just out of the way of traffic. When he regained consciousness, Josh checked the wetness he thought was blood at first. He checked over and over to see if he was hurt, as if he was missing a leg and just hadn't felt it yet. That's when he realized all his equipment was missing. The camera must have flown out the window. Then he spotted his DVDs, signed copies from the porn star he had been hanging out with that night. Slowly, Josh scrambled out of the destroyed vehicle and stood out in the wet shrubbery surrounding his car. There wasn't a scratch on him.

Moments later, emergency vehicles arrived. Paramedics checked Josh for any hidden injuries. A small crowd of uniformed San Diego

County personnel stood on the embankment of the freeway and muttered among themselves, "He should be dead."

Josh sat stunned. He was all right; nothing happened to him, not one scratch. As they waited for the tow truck, Josh frantically searched the bushes for his camera and the photos the porn star had given to him. He looked everywhere he could think that the stuff could have flown. Every angle. Every trajectory. Nothing.

When Josh returned home, dirty and wet, he crashed in his bed. He had lost his most important tool besides his computer. The next couple months only brought more frustration for Josh. True, the payments on his truck disappeared since his crash, but he still couldn't make any money. Josh had been in the middle of the most important job of his porn career. Sara, one of these girls on the banner at LA Erotica, had hired him as her webmaster and expected him to refurbish her website. But things had gone horribly. All joy disappeared with the crash. He couldn't think of anything else. Another photo designer he worked with on the site decided to quit abruptly and Josh felt hopelessly lost. All the while, Josh felt God pulling at his heart, showing him a better lifestyle if he would only just trust. So he decided to pull up his life as a web designer and get out.

He wrote Sara, "I feel like I'm hitting walls because this isn't what God wants me to do in life. I've been avoiding him for two years while trying without much success to get money the porn industry has to offer. I'm tired, my heart and soul hurt every night when I go to bed, and I know I should be on the other side of the fence."

Sara wasn't mad. She wasn't even disappointed. She wrote him back saying, "I want out too."

Whereas Josh had never really gotten his foot in the door in the porn business to where he made a lot of money, Sara was one of the more successful girls in the business and she wanted out despite her success.

Josh thought about moving to Arizona and be around his friend's church, possibly getting a job there in the design department. So he spent the next few days figuring a way to get out completely. That's how he found us. Josh stumbled onto our website and knew he had to talk to me. First he sent me an email:

Hey Craig,

Not sure what to say but I've been working freelance in the porn industry for about two years (and I'm still broke) and other than not getting anywhere money-wise it's really torn me apart inside. It's one thing to work in the porn industry and not believe in God, but my problem is I am a Christian. I had hopes of taking part of that 13 billion dollar a year industry and putting a few bucks in my pocket, but it didn't work too well and I'm tired . . . tired of working my butt off and not making any money, tired of turning my back on God and knowing he's watching me work around all this sin while trying to reason with myself that it's not that big of a deal, and I'm really tired of guys thinking what I do for a living is cool because if they only knew what it's like in the industry it would ruin their fantasy. So I'm not sure what I can do for you or where God wants me yet seeing as it's only been about four days since I decided to turn back around and go toward God. But I would really like to sit down and talk either on the phone or in person to hear what you goofballs have to say. =o) Anyway, I don't want to overload you too much and hope

```
this is enough general info. I'm just looking
for help and looking to help others.
     Josh (a former website designer for porn)
```

Before I even read the email, Josh tracked me down on the phone. I didn't have my phone number or personal contact information on the website, but he found a number of a friend of mine and called him to get hold of me. If he could be persistent with porn stars, then he could be so in getting in touch with me.

That week I happened to be speaking at The Flood, a college-aged church in San Diego. I told Josh to find me afterward so we could talk. After the group, we went to Denny's and had some sandwiches. We talked for three hours. Mostly about what Josh wanted to do with the rest of his life and how he wanted to get as far away from porn as possible.

I told him, "Get out now! If you even hang around these guys anymore or surround yourself in that atmosphere, you'll be sucked back in."

Josh decided then and there that he would go live with his friend in Arizona and forget about the porn business forever. But Josh hesitated with cutting all ties to his porn star friends. In the letter he wrote Sara he said, "I'm done with the porn business but I'm not disowning my friends in the industry. I'm still here for you in any way I can help as far as information goes. If you need to know where to look for something I'll tell you, or if you need help with your server I'll do that because I help all my friends out when I can. Also if you need someone just to listen so you can vent, or someone to talk to about faith and God, I'm here. I know your soul is hurting as much as mine is. I understand you have been in this business a long time and are entitled to what you deserve, but I also know it's tearing you up."

Sara never called Josh for more work on her internet server, but Josh kept in contact with another porn star named Trinity, a single mother with a daughter. Her real name was Michelle, and when she was nineteen she started as a porn star one night in a Las Vegas hotel. They talked her into having sex with Ron Jeremy, the most famous porn star in the business and she received $5,000 that night. She continued to do jobs and worked more and more while getting paid less and less. Eventually, Trinity became a prostitute at the Chicken Ranch, an establishment forty miles outside of Vegas where her fans could come and have sex with her. Josh and Trinity developed a close relationship. Although Trinity hated the work she had to do, she didn't want out because it would sacrifice her independence.

A couple months went by and LA Erotica was approaching fast. One night, Josh called me and told me he wanted to help us with our booths. He knew a lot of porn stars and wanted to distribute the message of "Jesus Loves Porn Stars." I told him that would probably be a bad idea for him, to surround himself with the very world he wanted to rid himself of. In fact, as he persisted, I told him in very strong terms not to come.

But he came anyway. Amidst all the hubbub and chaos of setting up our booths, Josh arrived and started taking XXXchurch flyers to all the porn stars he knew. He made quick rounds like a salesman, trying to get as many porn stars as he could to come by our booths and talk to us. He even attempted the mighty Jenna Jameson. He figured that if he could get her, then we would get a lot more attention. I admired his courage, but I kept telling him to leave.

As the day went by, I paid closer attention to exactly what he was doing. Along with our "Jesus Loves Porn Stars" flyers, he was handing out his black cards as well. I decided Josh needed to leave.

I approached him kind of heatedly. "What are you doing, Josh? I thought you wanted out."

"Yeah, but I think I could help these girls more if I did the work for them. They're going to have it done anyway and they might as well have somebody they can trust do it. Someone who will try and get them out of the business. Look what happened to Sara... she's out now," said Josh.

True, this girl was out, but I didn't buy Josh's act. Jimmy D, our pornographer friend, was shaking his head as he listened to our conversation. He saw a part of himself in young Josh. If only he could go back in time and be twenty-four again. If his financial circumstances were different, he might have made different choices. Josh wants to be in the mainstream too, and like Jimmy D, he doesn't have enough faith in himself to sacrifice or follow a dream through. So he settles.

I looked at Josh and saw him trying to justify his presence in the industry. He went around busily doing our work in order to compensate for the real work he wanted to do. Jimmy D felt bad as well, so he compensated. It was almost like, "If I can do some good things, maybe they will cancel out the bad." Jimmy D still films porn. He's conflicted but comfortable, so I don't see him leaving the business any time soon. But Josh hadn't gone too far with his profession. I could see him still cutting everything and going to Arizona, never to edit another porn site again. He could do what he really wanted.

"What do you think about Josh's goals?" I asked Jimmy D.

"He's not going anywhere."

The next day Josh brought Trinity by the booth. I didn't even know who she was at the time because Josh had never mentioned her before. I knew immediately that she was more to him than just a girl he felt needed to get out of the business.

"What's happened to Arizona, Josh?" I asked him later.

"It didn't work out," said Josh. "I think I'm going to move out to Las Vegas and live with Trinity."

What happened to his sign? He had the car crash and the Sara incident to show him that he could do much better than porn. I couldn't believe it, but Josh went to Vegas.

I didn't talk to him until a month later when I decided to find out how he was managing in his new apartment with his porn star girlfriend. I made the long hot summer drive to Vegas to see if Josh was really living the dream. I got there and he seemed like an entirely different person. Gone was the Josh who felt conflicted. Gone was the Josh who wanted to go to Arizona to get away from the porn business.

Their apartment was a wreck. I walked in and there was no furniture, only an air mattress and one couch. Josh had his computer set up on a small table with the hard drive and the insides gutted, laying everywhere. Boxes full of miscellaneous junk sat in the middle of the floor. Boxes full of porn sat next to the computer. The upstairs had no furniture anywhere either. One room was filled with the stuffed animals from Trinity's daughter, who was out of town with a friend. They planned on moving her in so she could be close to her mother, but the five-year-old girl was currently in Barstow, several hours away from the house while her mother stayed at the Chicken Ranch, a legal house of prostitution.

Trinity could make more money if people who saw her in porn could actually have sex with her. She supported Josh at this time because he had no job. He sat at home all day trying to learn how to be a better graphic designer and web editor. He had also lost contact with most of the girls he had been trying to set up with us.

I handed Josh the email that he first wrote me two months prior. He looked at it and did not recognize at first glance what it was. He read it quietly as I stood there and watched him. He then looked up at me and had nothing to say.

It took several minutes, but then it finally came out. Nothing but excuses. "Well, you don't know how hard it is, you don't understand. It is not that easy." One of the things he mentioned was that he did not want to wait till he was forty to have his first kid and be able to provide a steady income for his family. Josh was basically saying this is what he has to do so he can earn money and start a family someday. I strongly disagreed with him as he was headed back to San Diego the following week to file bankruptcy in a court of law.

Not only had Josh now moved in with a porn star and was trying desperately to drum up work in the industry, he was now employed by his girlfriend. He did not tell me his specific job title. I don't think he had one. He was just there for Trinity whenever she needed him.

On top of dropping stuff off to her at the ranch, Josh was also responsible for driving her back to Los Angeles for any upcoming porn shoots. Trinity did not have her driver's license and relied on Josh to get her from place to place. While I was there, Josh had to bring her some Gatorade. We made the drive at 2:00 in the morning out to the Chicken Ranch. The secluded brothel had girls stay there for weeks or months at a time. They couldn't leave for fear that they might contract AIDS, so they called it a prison.

Trinity and the other girls would have to line up in a cattle call in front of a mirror whenever a customer would enter the building. The customer sat on lavish couches while the man could see every inch of them. The purpose of the mirror was so he could see their backsides. He would pick one and she would take him into her private room. A bright lamp, too bright for reading, sat on their desks, so they could check for visible signs of STDs. If the customer was willing to pay more money, he could rent out bungalows in the back holding rooms.

As Josh drove me up that lonely road, a freak thunderstorm sent lightning across the sky. We talked some, but mostly sat in silence. He knew what I would tell him to do.

"So has Sara called you lately?" he asked. Why did Josh, who is in the middle of this huge mess himself, still care about Sara? After several minutes of discussion, it all made sense.

Josh and Sara were both planning on escaping the world of XXX. He still cared. I had almost concluded that Josh had become a different person. After my Denny's dinner with Josh, he apparently called Sara and asked to meet her outside of Porn Star Karaoke the following week. They met and discussed life for a few short minutes. Then Josh handed Sara my book that he had purchased from the resource table at The Flood the week before. He also wrote my name and my cell phone number on the inside cover.

Three days later she called me. As I was preparing to take my son to the zoo on a nice hot Saturday afternoon, I noticed a call on my cell phone—an 818 number. I answered and we talked. This was the first of several phone calls. Months later, Sara has completely removed herself from the porn industry after an eleven-year career. I filled Josh in on what had been going on with Sara. He was genuinely excited for her and I could tell he was glad to have played a role in that process.

But I didn't drive out to talk about Sara. I was concerned for Josh. For the next twenty minutes there was complete silence in the car. Josh was not willing to take a look at his own life. I commended him for his efforts in helping our ministry but at this point, I just saw it as a "feel good" for Josh so he could continue to carry on with his life, chasing his fantasies.

One thing that I have come to grips with over the last four years is that people first must desire to change and then be willing to take the steps necessary in order to change. Josh had me convinced that he wanted to change, but he was unwilling to make the right choices. So many people do the same thing as Josh. In the book of Romans, the apostle Paul says, "I want to do what is right, but it is sin inside me that makes me do wrong. When I want to do what is right, I seem to do what is wrong. I love God's law with all my heart, but there is another law that is at war with my mind. This law wins the fight and makes me a slave to sin. O what a miserable person I am!" (Romans 7:19–24a).

Josh gave Trinity her Gatorade that night. I saw then that he really did care for her, but he left knowing that she'd have sex with a stranger for money later that morning or the next day.

## ROCK BOTTOM

Four months after my trip to Las Vegas to see Josh, my phone rang at 4:30 in the morning on Saturday, October 30, 2005. My wife always gives me a hard time for keeping my phone on all the time. But this was different; this time I was the one bothered by the phone ringing. Who is calling me at this hour? Was there a death in my family? Or an emergency? I answered, and Josh was on the line.

As we talked on the phone that morning, it became clear to me that both Josh and Trinity had hit rock bottom. Trinity had enough of sex, enough of the faceless men using her for pleasure. She had decided that no financial independence was worth the slavery of her mind and body. Josh had enough of seeing the woman he cared for used at any hour of the day or night while he sat at home in a lonely apartment. They were ready to listen.

Not only would they listen, they needed help. It was a gutsy phone call on Josh's part, but he had enough trust in me to know I would understand. Josh told me that he married Trinity a month before and was truly in love with her and cared deeply about her daughter. After spending time with the both of them, I believed this was love. I know Josh and the girl he had feelings for was not the porn star Trinity but the girl Michelle.

Josh told me that Trinity was at the Chicken Ranch, but he wanted Michelle to come home for good. She had just wrapped up a couple movies in Los Angeles the week before to add to her catalog of over two hundred-plus adult films. But because the money was so bad these days for the work she had to do, she had to work at the Chicken Ranch more often to make the rent for their apartment.

Josh told me marriage had changed Michelle and him. It made them realize they were tired and worn out, and they wanted to escape. I pushed him that morning, truly trying to gauge if his desire to leave was real or was just another false alarm. This time it was different.

So what do we do next? We start over. Josh and Michelle and her daughter start a new life together. That is exactly what Christ can do for any of us no matter how far we have gone. For Josh and Michelle, a new start meant leaving Vegas and going home.

Josh's family recently had moved to Indiana. They agreed to let Josh and his new wife and daughter come live with them and help them get on their feet. Josh had lined up a job painting houses and was willing to get rid of his black business cards for good. He would paint—every day if he had to so Michelle could have a normal life. Michelle dreamed of opening her own hair salon one day. She knew that dream was far out of reach since cosmetology school took almost a year and close to $10,000 to complete. I told Josh that I would call him back later and try and put together a plan.

Three days later I sent out an email to the supporters of XXX church.com. Here is what it said.

We want to tell you about a girl named Trinity. We have started something called "The Trinity Project" based on a porn star that we are working with. We are trying to provide a path for her out of the industry. Trinity is a great person that we are raising funds to help provide a way out of the porn industry for.

Trinity has decided that she wants out for good! She is currently living in Las Vegas and has been doing porn and legalized prostitution for four years and has realized that this is not something she can do any longer.

Here is where you can play a part in this new life for Trinity. XXXchurch has ten days to make all this happen, so we are looking to you to help us out on this project. We plan on making a visit to Trinity in Las Vegas within the next two weeks and get Trinity packed up and moved to Indiana. She has family friends in Evansville, Indiana, whom she can live with who will help out with childcare as Trinity enrolls in cosmetology school. Her five-year-old daughter can get enrolled in first grade in Indiana. Indiana is a great place for Trinity to raise her daughter and she will be far away from all the temptations of the porn industry and the lifestyle she is leaving behind.

We have a list of things that we need to take care of to make this happen. We have told Trinity that we are going to do this for her if she agrees to leave the industry. Trinity will also be posting a blog on the XXXchurch site to keep everyone up to date on her progress. We also have some women from XXXchurch that are going to be communicating with Trinity.

So, here it is:

| | |
|---|---|
| U-Haul moving truck from Vegas to Indiana | $1,200 |
| Gas for U-Haul | $400 |
| Gas for other vehicle | $300 |
| Plane ticket for Trinity's daughter so she does not have to ride | $300 |
| Food and hotel on the road | $500 |
| Cost to terminate Las Vegas apartment lease | $700 |
| AVN booth space (Trinity was going to go to the porn show in January, she owes this money even though she will not go. She has agreed to put material in her booth about the Trinity Project) | $2,000 |
| Cosmetology school for eleven-month degree | $8,000 |
| Start-up money for Indiana | $1,000 |
| Total: | $14,400 |

Too often Christians spend their time praying, talking, and being spiritual with people, but never get in and get their hands dirty. The book of James says, "Faith without works is dead." Too many meetings. Too much political posturing. Too much condemnation. Too much inaction. Helping Trinity is a practical thing that calls people who think porn is a scourge on our society to step up to the plate and do something about it. Will you join us? All donations for the Trinity Project will go to helping Trinity and others in need like her.

God Bless!

XXXchurch.com

PS: Some of you might be asking yourself why we are helping a porn star who must have a lot of money. Let us clear up a few things. Jenna Jameson and a handful of porn stars make serious cash, while 90 percent of the girls in the industry are not making that kind of money. They stay in the industry because it is a sense of security and better money than working at Burger King. To put it in perspective for you: Trinity worked last week on two separate porn videos and made $900. The week before that she worked at the Ranch in Las Vegas prostituting herself and took home a check for $450 dollars. Is it worth it? No! We could go on and on and tell you what exactly she had to do for that money, but we won't. So if you are hung up on the money issue, please don't be. We have a chance to play a huge part in Trinity's life and that is what it is all about.

What happened next blew me away. My inbox was full of online donations adding up to $12,000 in less than three days. People were sending gifts, money, and encouraging emails. The emails made their way back to Josh and Michelle. For the first time they were recipients of the care and love of strangers rather than the abuse they were so used to receiving from the hands of strangers. For the first time, I believe they saw a glimpse of this abundant life that God wants to give each and every one of us. They realized that the sin and the world of porn that had consumed both of them was a cheap substitute for the love Christ wants to pour out on them. Within one week the $14,400 was raised from the supporters of XXXchurch.com.

One week later—let me say that again—one week later we hopped on a plane to Las Vegas to see Josh and Michelle one last time in Vegas. You might be deeply into porn or a lifestyle of sin, but you can escape. A week after Josh's phone call, he and his wife, Michelle, have committed to never going back.

Sunday, November 6, 2005, will be a day that I will never forget. That was the day Josh and Michelle said goodbye to Vegas and goodbye to porn and started their twenty-hour, cross-country journey to Indiana. Josh starts painting houses in a week. Michelle begins cosmetology school next month. As I stood in their garage as they drove away, I smiled. Later that night, back home sitting at my desk, I cried.

I don't cry much, but I could not stop this time. Four years of fighting porn. Four years of watching loved ones and my friends buy into the lie of pornography. For all that time I had watched an industry get bigger and bigger, but at that moment, I watched Josh help Michelle into a U-Haul van and drive away. For four years I'd asked myself whether it was worth it. I knew my answer.

Josh and Michelle are worth it! You are worth it! Your spouse is worth it! Your pastor is worth it! Your kids are worth it!

My hope and prayer is that we keep love out in front of people as we expose America's dirty little secret. God didn't ask me to create definitions or long drawn-out dissertations on the porn problem. He wanted one thing: conversation, getting to know those who have been affected by porn. So understand you have to make choices with your life, about what you think and what you do. If your definition of porn finds itself on a sliding gray scale, chances are you need to get up and start talking to someone about your dirty little secret. Or, if you can't see the hurting individuals behind porn, it's time to love them and allow them to talk to you about their secrets.

## ABOUT THE AUTHORS

### CRAIG GROSS

Craig Gross is the founder of XXXchurch.com, a ministry addressing issues most Christians today are too scared to talk about. Craig Gross is a sought-after voice in faith circles around the globe. With an almost cult following, Craig excites and challenges leaders of the church as well as mainstream laypeople to connect and grow with a God who loves everyone. Craig lives in Southern California with his wife, Jeanette, and their two kids, Elise and Nolan.

www.craiggross.com

### CARTER KRUMMRICH

Carter Krummrich resides in Newport Beach, California. He is working on his degree in Literary Journalism at University of California in Irvine and aspires to write for magazines. Carter has worked for the UC Irvine newspaper and interned for the *OC Weekly*, a local Orange County paper. Carter's parents encouraged him to step away from the family business of engineering and pursue dreams in writing and editing, and he loves reading and most sports, especially surfing.

www.carterkrummrich.com

ABOUT XXXCHURCH.COM

## XXXCHURCH.COM

XXXchurch is the brainchild of Craig and his good friend Mike Foster, who dreamed up the idea of this website over Chinese food one afternoon. XXXchurch exists to bring awareness, openness, accountability, and recovery to the church, society, and individuals in the issues of pornography and to begin to provide solutions through nonjudgmental and creative means. XXXchurch launched January 9, 2002, at the AVN Adult Expo in Las Vegas, Nevada, and has received over 45 million visitors to the website. The website and ministry has been covered by over a thousand news agencies from around the world, including CNN, *New York Times, World News Tonight, LA Times, Newsweek,* ABC, NBC, Playboy Channel, FOX, *GQ,* Comedy Central, and many others.

*www.XXXchurch.com*

## X3WATCH

Since the start of XXXchurch, the idea to develop free software was a huge priority. X3watch, released in November of 2002, is a free accountability program helping with online integrity. It is offered at no charge by the ministry of XXXchurch.com and its supporters. Whenever you browse the internet and access a site that may contain questionable material, the program will save the site name on your computer. Approximately every fifteen or thirty days (depending on your preference), a person of your choice (an accountability partner) will receive an email containing all possible questionable sites you have visited within the month. There is no other software on the market like X3watch that is available today for free. X3watch receives over a thousand new downloads a week, with over 170,000 users to date.

www.x3watch.com

## THE TRINITY PROJECT

We have met many people in the industry who dream of better things for their lives. However, many feel they don't have the resources or the means to pursue something other than porn. It's a job but it's not their future. XXXchurch is providing resources and custom plans for those who want out of the industry. Whether it is providing scholarships for school, helping with job placement, or addressing childcare issues, we want to provide opportunities out. It is the closing of the door on porn and the opening of a door to a new life. XXXchurch's focus has mainly been on sharing love, acceptance, grace, and truth with those who are in the industry, which has been very successful and powerful on many levels. As we have gotten to know more people and hear their personal stories, we felt compelled to get involved at a deeper level. To really help in whatever way we can. The name for the project came from Trinity, a porn star who we worked with to get out of the porn industry. She was the inspiration for this project.

To find out more about the Trinity Project or ways in which you can get involved, check out www.xxxchurch.com/getinvolved/trinity.asp.

## OTHER RESOURCES

www.integrity.com: the best filtered internet available
www.pureonline.com/xxxchurch: thirty-day online
counseling program
www.purelifeministries.org: live-in sexual addiction ministry

Thanks, Jeanette, for standing with me in this ministry.

Carter ... thanks for the time and passion you have put into this project and the ministry.

Ferebee ... thanks for believing in this project and helping me see it through.

Angela and Scott ... thank you for your willingness to take a chance on the porn guy and this book.

Junior and Rob ... thanks for your many reads of the manuscript and help with the proposal.

Luke Ford ... thanks for your kind words and attention to details.

The Diamond ... thanks for everything and no, you don't have to ship these books out.

Mars Hill Church ... thanks for Porn Sunday

Steve Gallagher, Joe Dallas, Brandon Cotter, Skip and Stacy at Integrity ... thanks for doing what you do.

1. "Porn Completey Destroyed Me," available at craigslist.com (anonymous writer).
2. Shawn Hubler, "Just the Facts of Life Now," *LA Times* (April 23, 2005).
3. Gil Reavill, *Smut: A Sex Industry Insider (and Concerned Father) Says Enough Is Enough* (East Rutherford, NJ: Penguin, 2005), 8.
4. Ibid., 4.
5. Ben Shapiro, *Porn Generation: How Social Liberalism Is Corrupting Our Future* (Washington, D.C.: Regnery, 2005), 1.
6. Amy Sohn, "A Laptop Never Says No: Online Porn Is Changing (Read 'Destroying') Relationships," *New York Magazine* (May 30, 2005).
7. Donald Miller, *"Searching for God Knows What....."*
8. Robert Lewis, *The Church of Irresistable Influence* (Grand Rapids: Zondervan, 2003.)